COLLI

CARD
GAMES

The Diagram Group

HarperCollins*Publishers*

HarperCollins Publishers
P. O. Box, Glasgow G4 0NB

A Diagram Book first created by
Diagram Visual Information Limited of
195 Kentish Town Road, London NW5 8SY,
England

First published 1991

Reprint 10 9 8 7 6 5 4 3

ISBN 0 00 458995 5

Printed in China

Introduction

Card playing has been a popular pastime among young and old for more than 500 years. This long history and the enormous variety of card games that exist give card playing its great potential as a plentiful source of entertainment for all ages.

The *Collins Gem Guide to Card Games* is a fascinating two-colour guide to the rules and strategies for more than 100 exciting family and children's games, from all-five to war, with mexicana, Black Maria, and Persian Pasha in between. There's something for everyone – beginner and expert alike. Also included is an easy-to-use, complete glossary of important terms used in card playing. And with each game, you'll find the answers to those inevitable debates over rules and scoring.

Most importantly, the book provides detailed instructions and play-by-play diagrams – illustrating techniques and surefire strategies – that will turn even the novice card player into an expert.

Created by the Diagram Group, the book is an attractive companion volume to the same team's *Collins Gem Guide to Family and Party Games*.

Contents

SECTION 1 FAMILY GAMES

All fives	9	Canasta variations
Auction pitch	12	*continued*:
Bezique	14	Samba
Bezique variations:	19	Combo-canasta
Three-handed		Casino 72
Rubicon		Casino variations: 80
Six-deck or Chinese		Royal
Eight-deck		Draw
Four-handed		Spade
Boston	27	Cribbage: 81
Bridge (contract)	32	Six-card
Bridge variations:	43	Five-card
Duplicate contract		Seven-card
Auction		Three-handed
Briscola	46	Four-handed
Calabrasella	49	Ecarté 89
Canasta	52	Euchre 92
Canasta variations:	58	Euchre variations: 95
Two-handed		Railroad
Cutthroat		Two-handed
Five-handed		Three-handed
Six-handed		Call-ace
Bolivian		Five hundred 97
Pennies from heaven		Five hundred variations: 101
Mexicana		For two players

Five hundred variations *continued*: For four players		Napoleon	143
		Napoleon variations:	145
		Purchase nap	
Forty-five	102	Seven-card nap	
Grand	106	Oh hell	146
Hearts	112	Pinochle	149
Hearts variations:	114	Pinochle variation:	154
Spot		Auction	
Black lady		Piquet	157
Greek		Piquet variations:	167
Domino		Piquet au cent	
Joker		Auction	
Heartsette		Pope Joan	170
For two		Preference	175
Black Maria		Rummy	178
Imperial	119	Rummy variation:	180
Klaberjass	126	Gin rummy	
Klaberjass variations:	131	Scotch whist	183
Three-handed		Seven up	186
Four-handed		Seven up variations:	188
Knaves	132	Four-handed	
Knaves variation:	134	California Jack	
Polignac		Skat	190
Loo:	136	Spoil five	199
Three-card		Vint	203
Five-card		Whist	207
Michigan	140		

SECTION 2 CHILDREN'S GAMES

Beggar my neighbour 212
Card dominoes 214
Cheat 216
  Up-and-down
Donkey 218
  Pig
Fish 220
Give away 222
Go boom 224
  Scoring go boom
  Crazy eights
Knockout whist 227
Linger longer 230
Memory 232
Menagerie 233
My ship sails 234

Old maid 235
  Le vieux garçon
Play or pay 237
Racing demon 239
Rolling stone 241
Sequence 242
Slap jack 244
Snap 246
  Easy
  Speed
Snip-snap-snorem 248
  Jig
Spit 250
Stealing bundles 252
War 254
  Persian Pasha

Glossary

BOODLE Cards carrying counters or money chips.

CANASTA Name of a game and of a meld of seven cards of the same rank made in that game.

CARTE BLANCHE A hand containing no court cards.

COURT CARDS The K, Q and J of each suit.

CUT Dividing a deck of cards into two parts after a shuffle, reversing the position of the two parts before dealing. Also a deck can be cut into several parts for making decisions by comparing the rank of cards revealed in the cut.

DEAL The method of giving players cards.

DECK Playing cards used for a particular game.

DEUCE The two of each suit.

DISCARD Card thrown away on the discard pile.

FOLLOW SUIT Playing a card of the same suit as the previous one.

GO KNOCKING Unable to play a card.

HAND The cards dealt and the play using those cards.

LEADING SUIT The suit of the first card played.

MELD A group of cards of the same rank or in sequence. Also, to lay out a group of cards or add one or more appropriate cards on an existing meld.

MISDEAL To deal cards incorrectly.

PACKET A group of two or more cards dealt together.

PASS When a player does not play or bid.

PIQUET DECK When all cards below the 7s are removed from the standard 52-card deck to form a 32-card deck.

RANK Order of cards or suits in play. Higher ranks take precedence over lower ranks.

REVOKE Failure to follow suit.

SEQUENCE A run of cards of the same suit.

SETBACK Penalty for not fulfilling a bid (of tricks).

SLAM Winning of all tricks by one player or side.

STOCK The cards remaining after the deal, used later in the game.

STRIPPING Removing certain cards from a standard deck of 52 cards.

SUIT Clubs, spades, hearts or diamonds.

TREY The three of each suit.

TRICK A group of cards, one from each player in turn according to the rules of the game.

TRUMP A suit that outranks all others. A trump card outranks any card from a plain suit.

UPCARD A card that is turned up, from the deal or the stock, to start a discard pile or to designate trumps.

WILD A card that can be used to replace any other card – e.g. joker and 2s are wild cards in canasta.

All fives

A game for two or three players similar to whist.

Cards

The standard deck of 52 cards is used with ace ranking high. A suit is assigned trumps which outranks all other suits. A set of two or three cards, one from each player in turn, is called a trick.

Aim

Individuals score points by trumping tricks.

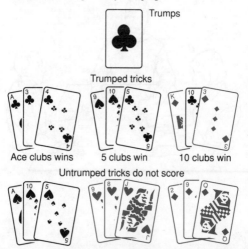

Trumps

Trumped tricks

Ace clubs wins   5 clubs win   10 clubs win

Untrumped tricks do not score

Preparing

Paper and pencil are needed for scoring. The player with the highest cut becomes dealer. Anyone may shuffle the pack before the cuts are made.

Dealing

The dealer shuffles the pack. Rotating clockwise and starting from the player on his left, he deals six cards in packets of three cards face down to each player. The next card is turned face up to assign trumps.

The dealer reveals the first trump suit.

By saying 'stand', the player to the left of the dealer accepts the assigned trumps and play begins. He says 'I beg' if instead he wants different trumps assigned. If the dealer decides to retain trumps, he says 'take one' and the player to his left then gains a point and starts play.

If the dealer decides to change trumps, he puts the upcard aside, deals a further packet of three cards to each player and turns up the next card to assign the new trumps. If the upcard is the same suit as before, the dealer repeats this process until a new trump is assigned. If the pack runs out, the next player to his left becomes dealer and begins the deal again.

Playing

The player to the left of the dealer places one card face up on the table. Players each follow suit with one card. The trick is taken by the person playing the highest ranking card; he leads for the next trick.

Scoring

Tricks are all turned face up at the end of the round. Only tricks containing certain trump cards score points, as follows:

Ace:	4 points
K:	3 points
Q:	2 points
J:	1 point
10:	10 points
5:	5 points

Winning the game

The player first reaching a score of 61 or more is the winner.

Auction pitch

Sometimes called setback, this variation of seven-up is
particularly popular in the USA.

Players

Two to seven people can play.

Cards

A standard deck of 52 cards is used. Ace ranks high. A
trick is two to seven cards, one played by each person
in turn.

Aim

Individuals try to score points to win the game.
Although seven points is the standard game, players
can play for 10, 11 or 21 points if they agree.

Preparing

Pencil and paper are needed for scoring.

Dealing

The dealer – chosen by the highest cut – shuffles the
cards and deals two packets of three cards, face down,
to each player.

Bidding

The player on the dealer's left either declares pass or
bids to make a score of one, two, three or four. The
last, a slam, is also known as 'shoot the moon' or
'smudge'.

The next player clockwise then passes or bids and so
on. Players must always bid higher than the previous
bidder, although the dealer may choose to take the last
bid over. The person holding the highest bid is known
as the pitcher.

Playing

The pitcher begins by playing one card face up, which also assigns trumps for that deal. Other players must follow the trump suit or make a discard. The trick is won by the highest ranking card and claimed by that player, who then leads for the next trick.

When the leading card is a plain suit, players can follow suit or play a trump card. If they cannot do either, they must discard one card.

Scoring

If the pitcher's score is equal to or greater than his bid, he keeps his score. If he has failed, he loses the number of points he bid, which may leave him with a minus score.

All other players score according to the cards they hold in their tricks.

Highest trump card:	1 point
Lowest trump card:	1 point
J of trumps:	1 point
Aces:	4 points
Ks:	3 points
Qs:	2 points
Js:	1 point
10s:	10 points
Highest total card value:	1 point

Winning the game

The person who first makes 7 or more points (or 10, 11 or 21, as agreed) wins the game. When players tie, points are counted in the order of high, low, J and then game. The pitcher always wins when he ties with another player.

Bezique

The history of bezique goes back 350 years, the standard game emerging from France. A derivation is pinochle, popular in the USA.

STANDARD BEZIQUE

Players

Standard bezique is for two players, but variations exist for three or four players.

Cards

Bezique is played with a 64-card double piquet deck – i.e. all cards below 7, except the ace, are removed from two standard 52-card decks.

One suit of a piquet deck

The ranking is ace (high), 10, K, Q, J, 9, 8, 7 (low).

Rank for bezique

high   low

Aim

Players try to gain the highest points total by making high-scoring tricks and declared melds.

Preparing

Pencil and paper are essential for scoring unless special bezique markers or a cribbage board are available.

Bezique marker

On a cribbage board each hole counts 10

Players agree whether the winning score shall be 1000 points or 2000 points.

Dealing

The dealer is chosen by the higher cut. Packets of three, two and three cards are dealt in three rounds to each player, making a hand of eight cards.

The next card is placed face up to assign trumps. If this

upcard is a 7, the dealer scores 10 points. A stock is made by placing all other cards face down.

Playing: stage one

The non-dealer leads by placing one card face up on the table. The dealer then completes the trick by adding any one of his cards.

The trick is claimed by the player who has placed the higher ranking card of the leading suit or a trump card. In the first stage, players do not have to follow suit and can use any trumps they hold.

If both people play the same card, the leading card wins the trick.

The winner of each trick may make one declaration, laying his declared meld face up on the table. The cards in a meld can also be used to make future tricks, as if they were still in the hand.

Melds and their points value are as follows:

a) Double bezique (500): two Qs of spades and two Js of diamonds.

b) Sequence (250): ace, 10, K, Q and J of trumps.

c) Any four aces (100).

d) Any four Ks (80).

e) Any four Qs (60).

f) Any four Js (40).

g) Bezique (40): Q of spades and J of diamonds.

h) Royal marriage (40): a K and Q of trumps.

i) Common marriage (20): a K and Q of the same non-trump suit.

j) Exchange (10): changing the up-card for the 7 of trumps. Whoever holds the other 7 of trumps gains 10 points when he plays it but it is not a declaration.

Cards in melds may be used for later declarations

providing they are not used in similar melds. For example, an ace already used in a four aces declaration cannot be used in a second meld of four aces.

Declarations when clubs are trumps

Trumps

a 500 points

b 250 points

c 100 points

d 80 points

e 60 points

f 40 points

g 40 points

h 40 points

i 20 points

j 10 points

Scores should be recorded as the game proceeds. After the winner has made his declaration he draws cards from the stock to replace those used. The other player then replenishes his hand from the stock. When the stock is used up, players proceed to stage two.

Playing: stage two

The last winner of a trick leads as players continue to make eight final tricks. Now they must follow suit with each leading card. Trumps may only be used when the lead cannot be followed. A player must win the trick if possible.

Play continues until players have used up their cards. The player winning the last trick gains 10 points.

When the game is complete, players gain 10 points for every brisque – i.e. an ace or a 10 contained in a trick.

Brisques

Penalties

1) Opponent scores 10 when a player draws out of turn.

2) Opponent scores 100 when a player holds more than eight cards.

3) A player forfeits 10 of his own points to his opponent when he plays to a trick after he has failed to draw a card during the first stage of play.

4) A player forfeits all eight tricks to his opponent in stage two if he fails to follow suit or take a trick.

Winning the match

The player to first reach 1000 or 2000 points, as agreed, is the winner.

BEZIQUE VARIATIONS

THREE-HANDED BEZIQUE

Three players play for themselves with three piquet decks (96 cards). The final aim is a score of 1500. Otherwise the game is the same as bezique.

RUBICON BEZIQUE

Two people play with four piquet decks (128 cards) and are dealt nine cards singly or in packets of three.

Trumps are assigned by the first sequence or marriage that is declared. Stock cards are not turned up and the 7 of trumps has no value.

Playing proceeds as in standard bezique. The last trick, however, is worth 50 points, and there are four additional types of declaration, as follows:

a) Quadruple bezique (4500): four Qs of spades and four Js of diamonds.

b) Triple bezique (1500): three Qs of spades and three Js of diamonds.

c) Back door or ordinary sequence (150 points): ace, 10, K, Q and J of a non-trump suit.

d) Carte blanche (50): declared by a player who has been dealt a hand without court cards. He displays the carte blanche and draws a card from the stock. Unless this is a court card, he can declare carte blanche again and score a further 50 points. This continues until he draws a court card.

Rubicon declarations when clubs are trumps

a 4500 points

b 1500 points

c 150 points

d 50 points

Cards in rubicon melds may be used to make similar combinations. If a Q is played from a meld containing four Qs, for example, another Q can be added to make four Qs again. Also, two more marriages can be made by rearranging two other marriages of the same suit.

Brisques are ignored unless there is a tie or a player is about to be rubiconed for failing to make 1000 points. Both players' brisques are then counted.

Winning the game

After one deal, the player with the higher score gains 500 points plus the difference between his own and his opponent's score.

When the loser is rubiconed, his score is nil and the winner gains 1000 points plus 320 for all brisques and the sum of his own and his opponent's score.

If both players have scored less than 1000 points, the one with the higher score is still the winner and gains as above.

The winner gains an extra 100 points if his opponent has scored less than 100 during the game.

If players' scores are close, fractions of 100 points may be taken into account. Otherwise, they are ignored.

SIX-DECK BEZIQUE OR CHINESE BEZIQUE

This game is similar to rubicon bezique but played with six piquet decks (192 cards) and a hand of 12 cards each, dealt singly or in packets of three.

Trumps are assigned by the first declared sequence or marriage. Brisques are never counted. The last, winning trick scores 250 points.

Declarations are as in rubicon bezique, plus five more in the trump suit. Also, carte blanche scores 250. Six-

deck declarations (in trumps) and their points value are:
a) four aces (1000)
b) four 10s (900)
c) four Ks (800)
d) four Qs (600)
e) four Js (400)

Six-deck declarations when spades are trumps

a 1000 points

b 900 points

c 800 points

d 600 points

e 400 points

A bezique is declared according to the trump suit

| Trumps hearts | Trumps diamonds | Trumps clubs | Trumps spades |

Winning the game

Scores are made after a single game as for rubicon except the winner's bonus is 1000 points and a player is rubiconed for a score less than 3000, not 1000.

EIGHT-DECK BEZIQUE

Eight-deck declarations when clubs are trumps

a 9000 points

b 2000 points

c 1800 points

d 1600 points

e 1200 points

f 800 points

g 50 points

Played as six-deck but with eight piquet decks (256 cards) and a hand of 15 cards each. Declarations are similar to six-deck declarations with differences (and points values) as listed:

a) Quintuple bezique (9000)
b) Five trump aces (2000)
c) Five trump 10s (1800)
d) Five trump Ks (1600)
e) Five trump Qs (1200)
f) Five trump Js (800)
g) Bezique (50)

With a score less than 5000 a player is rubiconed.

FOUR-HANDED BEZIQUE

Four-handed declarations with diamonds as trumps

a 40,500 points

b 13,500 points

c 1000 points

d 900 points

e 800 points

f 600 points

g 400 points

h 500 points

Similar to rubicon bezique but played with six piquet decks (192 cards) and each player is dealt nine cards. Players pair up, with partners sitting opposite each other.

After winning a trick a player may declare or may give his partner the option of declaring. A player may use his partner's declared cards in his own melds.

Scoring is similar to rubicon bezique with differences as listed:

a) Sextuple bezique (40,500)

b) Quintuple bezique (13,500)

c) Any four aces (1000)

d) Any four 10s (900)

e) Any four Ks (800)

f) Any four Qs (600)

g) Any four Js (400)

h) Double carte blanche (500): both partners dealt hands without court cards.

Boston

A variation of whist which was popular during the American Revolution.

Players

Four people play individually. Sitting positions can be agreed by cutting the deck, each person choosing their place in order.

Cards

Two standard 52-card decks are required. The one not used in play is used to select the rank order of suits known as preference, colour and plain. Ace ranks high. A trick is a set of four cards, one played in turn by each person.

Rank

Aim

Players score by making and fulfilling bids.

Preparing

A number of chips are needed for scoring. Each person begins with the same number. (Some authorities recommend 1000 each in fives, tens, twenties and fifties, to make settlement easier.) Before the first deal, each player puts 10 chips into the pool. If the pool contains more than 250, excess chips are put aside and added to the next pool.

Dealing

The first dealer is chosen by high cut, ace ranking low.
The whole of one pack is shuffled and dealt clockwise
in four packets of three followed by a single card to
each player. The dealer forfeits 10 of his chips to the
pool if he misdeals, and the deal passes to the player on
his left.

Ranking the suits

The second deck of cards can then be shuffled by
anyone before being cut in half by the player opposite
to the dealer. He then turns up the top card of the
bottom half, which assigns the preference suit. The suit
of the same colour is called the colour suit and the
other two are plain suits.

Cutting for preference

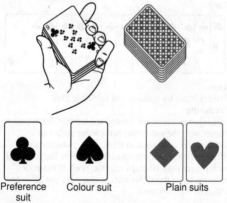

| Preference suit | Colour suit | Plain suits |

Bidding

The player to the dealer's left begins by passing or bidding. Each player makes a bid in turn, clockwise. Except for no trump bids, a player chooses his own trumps but usually waits until his bid is accepted before declaring it.

The bids have a rank order from **a** (low) to **m** (high), each one outbidding those above it, as follows:

a) Boston: make five tricks declaring one of the plain suits as trumps.

b) Make six tricks.

c) Make seven tricks.

d) Little misery: lose 12 tricks, with no trumps. Before play each person discards one card face down.

e) Make eight tricks.

f) Make nine tricks.

g) Grand misery: lose all 13 tricks with no trumps.

h) Make 10 tricks.

i) Make 11 tricks.

j) Little spread: lose 12 tricks, with no trumps and the hand of cards face up on the table.

k) Make 12 tricks.

l) Grand spread: lose all 13 tricks, with no trumps and the hand of cards face up on the table.

m) Grand slam: make all 13 tricks.

If two or more players bid to make the same number of tricks, the trump suit they each choose is ranked preference suit (high), colour suit and plain suit (low), thus ranking their bids.

Passing

If all four players pass, everyone discards their hands and adds 10 chips to the pool. A new shuffle and deal is made by the person to the dealer's left.

Playing

The player who made the highest bid aims to fulfil his bid, while the other players attempt to prevent him. The player to the left of the dealer leads by laying a card face up on the table. The others must follow suit if possible and may only trump or play another suit if they have no cards in the leading suit.

Revoking

A player who fails to follow suit is said to revoke. Anyone who revokes must pay 40 chips into the pool and lose his hand.

Settlement

When all 13 tricks have been made, accounts are settled.

1) The player who fulfils his bid is paid by each of the other players. If his bid was for seven or more tricks, he also gets the pool.

2) The player who fails to make his bid number of tricks pays the other players. He must also double the number of chips in the pool.

Fulfilled bids to make tricks are paid according to table **A**.

Failed bids to make tricks must pay according to table **B**.

The number of tricks by which a player fails to fulfil his bid are called the 'number put in for'.

Bids to lose tricks pay or are paid according to table **C**. The one who fails pays all players, or all players pay the one who fulfils his bid.

TABLE A

Tricks bid	5	6	7	8	9	10	11	12	13
Payment	10	15	20	25	35	45	70	120	180

TABLE B

Number put in for	Tricks bid								
	5	6	7	8	9	10	11	12	13
					Payment				
1	10	15	20	25	35	45	70	120	180
2	20	25	30	35	45	55	80	130	200
3	30	35	40	45	55	70	95	145	220
4	40	45	50	55	65	80	110	160	240
5	50	55	60	70	80	95	125	180	260
6		65	70	85	95	110	140	200	280
7			80	100	110	125	155	220	300
8				115	125	140	170	240	320
9					140	155	185	260	340
10						170	200	280	360
11							220	300	390
12								320	420
13									450

TABLE C

Bid	Payment
Little misery	20
Grand misery	40
Little spread	80
Grand spread	160

Bridge

Bridge emerged in 1896, a development from the older game of whist. Auction bridge evolved in 1904, and in 1925, contract bridge was formulated and soon became the most popular form of bridge.

CONTRACT BRIDGE

Players

Four people play in pairs. Partners sit opposite to each other and are called north-south and east-west respectively.

Cards

The game calls for the standard deck of 52 cards. Ace ranks high. The 2 is known as deuce and the 3 trey.
A second deck with different backs is often shuffled while the deal takes place, in preparation for the next deal.

A set of four cards, one played in turn by each person, is called a trick.

During the bidding, suits are ranked spades (high), hearts, diamonds and clubs (low).

Honours are the four aces when there are no trumps. When there are trumps, honours are the ace, K, Q, J and 10 of trumps.

Rank

high   low

No trump honours

Honours when clubs are trumps

Rank of suits

high   low

Aim

A partnership aims to win the most points in the best of three games, known as a rubber.

Preparing

One deck is spread face down, from which each player draws one card. Those with the two highest cards become partners, as do the two who draw the two lowest cards.

The player holding the highest card becomes the dealer and chooses where to sit, with his partner sitting opposite. If cards of the same value are drawn, they are ranked by suit.

Any player can shuffle the cards before the dealer
makes the final shuffle and invites the player on his left
to cut. Meanwhile, the dealer's partner shuffles the
second deck.

Bridge score pads and pencils are required.

We	They

**Scoring pad for
contract bridge**

Dealing

Beginning with the player on the dealer's left, the cards
are dealt singly, face down in clockwise rotation, until
each player has 13 cards.

Bidding

When everyone has examined the cards in their hands
the auction is begun by the dealer. The other players call
in turn in clockwise rotation.

A player can call bid, pass, double or redouble:

a) A pass means a player does not wish to bid; he can
make another call later. If all four players pass in the
first round of the auction, all cards are thrown in and the
person to the left of the dealer shuffles and deals
again. When three passes follow a bid, double or
redouble, the auction ends.

b) A player who bids calls the number of tricks in excess of six that his partnership will make in a stated trump suit or in no trumps. For example, calls of 'two clubs' or 'five no trumps' means the player believes his partnership can make eight tricks with clubs as trumps, or 11 tricks with no trumps.

Each bid must be higher than the one before it by the player calling a larger number of tricks or a higher ranking trump suit. 'No trumps' ranks highest of all.

The rank order of some sample bids would be:

1) seven no trumps (highest possible call; known as a grand slam)
2) six no trumps (known as a small slam)
3) five diamonds
4) four no trumps
5) four spades
6) four hearts
7) four diamonds
8) four clubs
9) three clubs
10) one clubs (lowest possible call)

c) A player calls double when he believes he could prevent the previous bid from being made if it became the contract. The bid can be outbid by any player as normal, in which case it does not become the contract. However, if a doubled bid does become the contract, the scores are doubled by the winners if they fulfil their contract or by the partnership that called double if the contract is not fulfilled.

d) When their bid has been doubled, one of the bidding partnership may call redouble, reasserting their confidence in their bid. A bid that has been redoubled can be outbid by either partnership.

The contract

The partnership from which the highest call came in the auction now has to fulfil that contract during play. Their opponents aim to prevent them.

The declarer

The member of the contracting partnership who first bid no trumps or a trump suit (spades, hearts, diamonds, clubs), is called the declarer and plays both hands. His partner, called the dummy, lays his hand on the table when the lead card has been played. He takes no further part in the play of that deal.

Sample deal and bidding

```
                     ♠ 8 6
                     ♥ J 10 7 6
                     ♦ A Q 9 8 6 4 3
                     ♣
West leads
♠ A 5 4 3          ┌─────────┐          ♠ K Q J 9 7 2
♥ 8 5              │    N    │          ♥ 3 2
♦ J 10          W  │         │  E        ♦ 5 2
♣ K 8 7 6 5        │    S    │          ♣ 10 9 4
                   └─────────┘
                     ♠ 10
                     ♥ A K Q 9 4
                     ♦ K 7
South is dealer      ♣ A Q J 3 2
```

Bidding

S	→	W	→	N	→	E
1♣		double		1♦		1♠
2♥		2♠		3♦		double
3♥		pass		pass		3♠
4♥		pass		pass		pass

The contract is four hearts to be made by North-South. South is the declarer. North and his hand are the dummy. His cards are placed face up on the table, trumps to his right and other suits ranked in rows.

The dummy hand laid down by North

Playing

The first player is the person to the left of the dealer. When the bidding is complete, he leads by playing any card from his hand face up on the table. The trick is completed by each person playing one card in turn, clockwise. The declarer plays a card from his own hand and from the dummy hand in correct order. He must play the first card he touches, except when rearranging the hand.

Every card must follow the leading suit. Only if a player is unable to follow suit may he play a card from another suit.

Winning the trick

1) When the contract is a no trump bid, all suits are ranked equally, so the highest card in the leading suit wins the trick.

2) When the contract is a bid in trumps, either the highest card in the leading suit or, if any trumps are played, the highest trump card wins the trick.

The winner of one trick leads the next trick.

Some winning tricks

Diamonds lead, no trumps, 10 of diamonds wins

Spades lead, clubs trumps, 5 of clubs wins

Tricks are gathered in piles of four cards, face down in front of the declarer in the contracting partnership and either player of the other pair.

Tricks are piled to show how many have been made. Any trick can be inspected before the inspecting partnership plays in the next trick.

Fulfilling the contract

The contracting partnership is said to have 'made the book' when their first six tricks are taken. They must then make at least the number of tricks they bid. The tricks in the book are piled together so that the extra tricks can be clearly counted.

Scoring

Both partnerships should keep scores to avoid disputes. Scores also affect the strategy of the game. A horizontal line is drawn across the WE (one partnership) and the THEY (the opponents) columns. Points can be scored 'below the line' and 'above the line'.

1) Below the line (trick points): Only the declarer's partnership scores trick points if they have fufilled the contract for the hand. Only the extra tricks are scored below the line.

2) Above the line (premium points): Both sides score premium points if they achieve any of the following in the hand:

overtricks (tricks over the number bid);

doubling or redoubling successfully;

making a slam that was bid;

honour cards dealt in the hand;

winning the final game of a rubber; or

undertricks, which the declarer's partnership fails to make to complete their contract. Their value is added to the opponent's score.

A partnership is said to be vulnerable when its first game towards a rubber has been won. When the score is one game all, both partnerships are vulnerable.

Winning the game

Progress towards winning a game is shown by the number of trick points; 100 or more wins a game. More than one hand may be played.

After each hand, a horizontal line is drawn below the trick scores of both partnerships. Scoring tricks for the next game begins from zero, below this line. Premium scores continue above the line without division.

Winning the rubber

The first side to win two games scores 700 premium points if the opponents have not won a game, 500 if they have. The rubber is won by the partnership with the higher total of combined trick and premium points.

Back scoring

In a competition where partners rotate, the status of an individual is calculated by back scoring after each rubber:

1) the losing partnership's score is deducted from the winner's to find the difference;

2) the difference is rounded up to the nearest 100 – for example, 750 becomes 800;

3) the rounded difference is divided by 100 – for example, 800 becomes eight; and

4) the winning partners are given a plus score for the rubber (for example, plus eight). The losers get the same minus score (minus eight).

Winning the competition

As individuals play further rubbers with different partners, they acquire plus or minus scores. At the end of the competition, the player with the highest plus score is the overall winner.

Recording scores on the scoring pad

We	They
70	

We	They
150	
70	
30	

a) WE score 70 trick points.

b) WE score 30 trick points and 150 premium points.

WE win the first game (100 trick points) and a line is
drawn across both columns. WE are now vulnerable.

c

We	They
150	200
70	
30	

d

We	They
	150
150	200
70	
30	
	60

c) WE fail to make a contract by two tricks. THEY
score 200 vulnerable undertrick points.

d) THEY score 60 trick points and 150 premium points.

Scoring table for contract bridge
Declarer's below-the-line trick scores ♣ ♦ ♥ ♠ NT

First extra trick (over six) bid and made	20 20 30 30 40	
Subsequent tricks bid and made	20 20 30 30 30	
Doubling (double the trick score)		
Redoubling (double the doubled score)		

Above-the-line scores	**Not vulnerable**	**Vulnerable**
Small slam	500	750
Grand slam	1000	1500
Undoubled overtrick	Trick value	Trick value
Doubled overtrick	100	200
Redoubled overtrick	200	400
Fulfilling a doubled or redoubled contract	50	50

Rubber, game and partscore

	Points
Winning rubber (opponents have no game)	700
Winning rubber (opponents have one game)	500
Winning one game in unfinished rubber	300
Having the only partscore in unfinished rubber	50

Honours (in one hand)

	Points
Four trump honours	100
Five trump honours	150
Four aces (no trump contract)	150

Undertricks

	a	b	c
First trick (not vulnerable)	50	100	200
Subsequent tricks	50	200	400
First trick (vulnerable)	100	200	400
Subsequent tricks	100	300	600

a = undoubled

b = doubled

c = redoubled

BRIDGE VARIATIONS

DUPLICATE CONTRACT BRIDGE

An advanced form of bridge – the only one played in international tournaments – in which several groups of players, in turn, receive the same deal of cards, thus testing skill rather than luck.

AUCTION BRIDGE

Auction bridge lies between whist and contract bridge in the evolution of the game. The rules are the same as for contract bridge, but the scoring is different, which affects the players' strategy.

The main differences in the method of scoring are:

1) Vulnerability does not exist, so there is no extra penalty for failing to fulfil a contract when one partnership has already won a game.

2) Odd tricks – i.e., more than the book of six – are scored below the line whether or not they were contracted for and count toward winning the game if the declarer has at least fulfilled the contract.

Scoring trick points

	♣ ♦ ♥ ♠ NT
Undoubled	6 7 8 9 10
Doubled	12 14 16 18 20
Redoubled	24 28 32 36 40

Winning the game
The partnership that first scores 30 points below the line wins that game, and a line is drawn across the score pad, as in contract bridge.

Winning the rubber
The first partnership to win two games wins that rubber and gains 250 extra points.

Scoring conventions
Three or more honours in the trump suit, or three or more aces in no trumps, earn points (scored above the line) for the partnership that holds them, whichever partnership it is. The honours score as follows:

Three honours (or aces):	30 points
Four honours (or aces) divided:	40
Five honours divided:	50
Four honours in one hand:	80
Five honours divided four to one:	90
Four aces in one hand:	100
Five honours in one hand:	100

If a partnership bids and fulfils a doubled contract, the declarer scores 50 bonus points above the line and 50 points for every trick above the contracted number.

If a redoubled contract is bid and made, declarer's side gains 100 bonus points and 100 points for each trick exceeding the contract.

The opponents acquire points above the line for each trick the declarer's partnership fails to make (undertrick), as follows:

Undoubled contract: 50
Doubled contract: 100
Redoubled contract: 200

Whatever the contract bid, a small slam (12 tricks), made by either side, scores 50 points above the line and a grand slam (13 tricks) scores 100 points.

Briscola

A partnership game of Italian origin, briscola is popular among Italian-Americans in the USA.

Players

Four people play in pairs. All players cut the cards for partners; the two with the highest cut become partners and choose sitting positions, which must be opposite each other. The other two become partners and sit in the remaining places. Either player from the partnership with the higher cut becomes the first dealer.

Cards

A deck of 40 cards is made from the standard 52-card deck by removing the 8s, 9s and 10s.

The cards rank ace (high), 3, K, Q, J, 7, 6, 5, 4 and 2 (low).

A set of four cards, one played in turn by each person, is called a trick.

Rank for briscola

high   low

Aim

Partners aim to score 121 points or more, in two or more hands, by making tricks with high-scoring cards.

Dealing

The dealer shuffles the cards. Starting with the player on the dealer's right, three cards are dealt singly, face down, counterclockwise.

The next card is placed face up and becomes the upcard. The remaining cards are placed face down in a pile to form the stock.

The trump suit for the hand is that of the upcard.

Playing

The player to the right of the dealer leads by placing one card from his hand on the table. Each player, in turn counterclockwise, lays out one card face up. Cards do not have to follow suit.

The trick is won either by the highest trump card or the highest ranking card from the leading suit.

When a trick has been won, each player takes the top card from the stock, in turn counterclockwise, beginning with the person who won the trick. That player leads for the next trick.

Play continues until the stock is exhausted. At this point scores for the first hand are totalled and a second hand is dealt and played, as above.

Conventions

The upcard is the last card to be taken, after which partners can inspect each other's hands before playing for the final tricks.

After partners have made their first trick, they are permitted to give each other information, using facial and hand signals, about which cards they hold. Sometimes signals are used to misinform their opponents.

Scoring and winning the game

The maximum score for one hand is 120. The first
partnership to reach a score of 121 wins the game. If
partners think they have reached 121 points during the
second hand, they can throw in their hands. If their
total is not 121, however, their opponents win the
game.

Table of card values

Aces: 11 points
3s: 10 points
Ks: 4 points
Qs: 3 points
Js: 2 points

All other cards have no points value.

Calabrasella

A fast-moving game for three players, two playing against one.

Cards

The 8s, 9s and 10s are removed from a standard 52-card deck to leave a deck of 40 cards, ranked in an unusual way. Three cards, one in turn from each player, makes a trick. There are no trumps.

Ranking for calabrasella

high   low

Aim

Individuals score points by making tricks.

Preparing

Each player may start with a set of an agreed number of counters; between 200 and 500 is recommended. Paper and pencil may be needed for scoring if counters are not used.

Dealing

The players cut the cards. The one with the lowest cut shuffles and deals 12 cards to each player, face down in packets of four. The deal proceeds clockwise.

The last four cards are piled face down and are known as the widow.

Bidding

Everyone in turn, beginning with the player to the left of the dealer, chooses to play or to pass. If all three pass, the cards are thrown in and there is a new deal. The first player who bids to play will do so alone against the other two, who play as partners for that hand.

The widow

Before play begins, the single player can exchange up to four of his cards with cards from the widow. If he does, the discards remain piled face down on the widow. The cards he takes into his hand must be laid face up on the table. The player who takes the last trick will take these four remaining cards.

Playing

The player on the dealer's left leads, followed by the other two players in turn clockwise. If they cannot follow suit, they must discard. The person playing the highest ranking card of the leading suit wins the trick. Players in the opposing partnership keep their tricks together.

Scoring

Players each score the value of the cards in their tricks. The side who takes the last trick adds the card value of the four cards in the widow and an extra three points. The maximum score is 35 points.

The final score for the hand is the difference between the total points of the two sides – i.e., between the single player and the partnership.

The values of cards are aces: 3 points; 3s, 2s, Ks, Qs and Js: 1 point each.

When the single player wins, the opponents each pay him his final score in counters.

When the partnership wins, the single player pays each of them the final score for the hand.

Winning the game

Play continues until one player has lost all his counters, the winner then being the one with most counters left. If playing for points, the payoff is made in points instead of counters, and the winner is the one who first makes 100 points. In this case, some players will make negative scores.

Canasta

A game from the rummy family, canasta was
developed in Uruguay and passed via Argentina to the
USA in 1949, where its popularity peaked in the 1950s.

Players

Four people play and score in pairs. Two or three
people can also play individually.

Cards

The canasta deck of 108 cards consists of any two
standard decks of 52, plus four jokers. Cards are not
ranked but have points values (see table).

Table of points values of cards

Card by denomination	Points value and name
Red 3 (diamond and heart)	100 Bonus card
	800 (if a pair hold four)
Joker	50 Wild card
Deuce (2)	20 Wild card
Ace	20 Natural card
8, 9, 10, J, Q, K	10 Natural cards
4, 5, 6, 7	5 Natural cards
Black 3 (club and spade)	5 Stop card

Melds

Three or more cards make a meld, which must contain:
1) only cards of the same denomination;
2) at least two natural cards;
3) not more than three wild cards;
4) no red 3s; and
5) no black 3s unless the player is going out.

A meld of seven cards is called a canasta, which can be
natural or mixed and attracts bonus points.

Examples of some melds

a) three natural cards
b) three natural and two wild cards
c) a natural canasta of seven natural cards
d) a mixed canasta of four natural and three wild cards

Aim

To be the first pair to gain 5000 points.

Preparing

Paper and pencil are needed for scoring. A score-keeper is chosen by consensus, or a non-player may take the job. All players cut the canasta deck, the cards ranking normally with ace high and suits ranking spades high, hearts, diamonds and clubs. Anyone cutting a joker cuts again.

The two highest and the two lowest cuts form partnerships. The player with the highest cut chooses the final seating position and makes the first deal. Partners sit opposite each other.

The dealer shuffles the cards and invites the player on his left to cut the cards.

Dealing

Beginning with the player to the dealer's left, cards are dealt singly and face down clockwise. When everyone has 11 cards, the undealt cards are piled face down to form the stock.

The discard pile is begun by turning the top card from the stock face up on the table. If this upcard is wild or a red 3, the next card is turned up and placed across the discard pile, freezing it.

Playing

The person to the dealer's left begins play, which continues in clockwise rotation. Each player draws the top card from the stock, makes any possible melds (or adds to those of his partner) and finally places a card in the discard pile. The procedure is as follows:

1) Any red 3s held in the hand must be laid out face up and replaced with cards from the stock.

2) The first meld of the deal must reach a value fixed by the partnerships' accumulated score (see table).

3) Any canasta melded is gathered into a pile. A red card is put on top of a natural canasta and a black card on top of a mixed one.

4) More cards may be added to the partnership's existing canastas except that a fourth wild card cannot be added to a mixed canasta and no wild card can be added to a natural canasta.

Table A

Accumulated score from previous deals	Minimum value of first meld of next deal
3000 upwards	120
1500 to 2995	90
0 to 1495	50
minus score	15

The discard

If it is not frozen, the discard pile can be acquired as follows:

1) A player of a partnership that has already laid out melds may take the upcard instead of one from the stock if his hand contains at least two natural cards of the same value as the upcard.

2) The upcard must then be melded by adding it to two natural cards or to one of the partnership's existing melds.

(It is generally accepted that the upcard cannot be added to a canasta. Also, the old ruling allowed it to be added to a natural and a wild card, but this is not usual in modern play.)

3) The whole of the discard pile may then be taken into the player's hand.

4) As many cards as possible are then used from the hand to add to melds or make new ones. Any red 3 picked up in the discard must be laid out.

5) One card is finally thrown away, as in basic play. If the stock pile runs out, the remaining discard pile is turned face down to use as stock.

A discard pile is frozen and cannot be picked up:

a) by a partnership that has not made the first meld of the deal;

b) by a player whose turn it is when the upcard is a black 3 (the pile is unfrozen when he throws his discard on it); or

c) by any player when the upcard is a wild card or red 3. All discards are then put across the pile until someone unfreezes it by melding a subsequent upcard card with two natural cards.

The frozen discard

with black 3

with a wild card (joker)

Ending play

A player wanting to go out at his next turn usually asks 'may I go out partner?' so his partner can take appropriate action. The reply may be yes or no, and must be obeyed.

Any player can go out by melding all his cards, providing he lays down a canasta or his partnership has already made one. Three or four black 3s may be melded together only to go out and may not be melded with wild cards.

Going out concealed happens when a player has not melded any cards on the table before his final turn.

Scoring

In addition to the denomination value of the cards, bonus points and penalty points are allotted.

One to three red 3s:	+100 each
Four red 3s:	+800
Going out:	+100
Going out concealed:	+200
Natural canasta:	+500
Mixed canasta:	+300

If a partnership has not made a first meld, there are penalties for holding red 3s, as follows:

Holding one to three red 3s:	-100 each
Holding four red 3s:	-800
Failing to reveal a red 3:	-200

Recording the scores

Each partnership should have a plus and a minus column on the score sheet.

A partnership's plus column should include:

1) total value of cards in melds;
2) bonus for going out;
3) bonus for mixed canastas;
4) bonus for natural canastas; and
5) bonus for red 3s.

A partnership's minus column should include:

1) total value of cards still held at end of play; and
2) any penalty points.

The total of minus points is deducted from the plus total to give the partnership's score.

Winning the game

Hands are played until one partnership reaches 5000 points.

CANASTA VARIATIONS

Canasta is adaptable for any number of players from two to six. It is an exciting game of strategy; the variations selected here offer many strategic alternatives. They are played to standard canasta rules with modifications as described for each variation.

TWO-HANDED CANASTA

Each player is dealt 15 cards. During play two cards are drawn from the stock and one is discarded. Two canastas must be melded before going out.

CUTTHROAT CANASTA

This is the standard game played by only three people, each playing for himself with a hand of 11 cards. The following modifications to the standard rules are optional.

Playing

At each turn, two cards are drawn from the stock and one discarded. Each person plays for himself until one person takes the discard pile. This player then continues to play alone, and the other two join forces in partnership against him.

When a player goes out without anyone having taken the discard, he scores as the lone player against the partnership of the other two.

If the stock is exhausted before anyone goes out, play ends after the player who drew the last stock card has discarded.

The value of a starting meld may be different for each partner, according to his accumulated score.

Cutthroat partnership

Scoring
Red 3s count for individual players; otherwise the partnership score is credited to both partners. The game is won by the player who first reaches a score of 7500 points.

FIVE-HANDED CANASTA
Played in partnerships exactly as standard four-handed canasta. One side has three players, who take turns to sit out at each deal.

SIX-HANDED CANASTA
There are either two partnerships of three players seated A B A B A B, or three partnerships of two seated A B C A B C.

Six-handed partnerships

Partnership A plays
against partnership B

A, B and C
partnerships play
against each other

A deck of 162 cards is used – i.e., 3 x 52 plus 6 jokers.
Each player is dealt 13 cards.
A score of 10,000 wins the game.
When a partnership's score reaches 7000, its initial
meld must be worth 150 points.
Up to four red 3s count 100 points each. Five red 3s
count 1000, and all six red 3s count 1200.
To go out, two canastas must have been melded by the
partnership.

BOLIVIAN CANASTA

A partnership game for four people, played as standard
canasta with the following differences.

Cards

A deck of 162 cards is used – i.e., 3 x 52 plus 6 jokers.
Each player is dealt 15 cards. Two cards are drawn
from the stock at each turn and one discarded.

Aim

To win the game by scoring 15,000 points.

Value of opening melds

Score of side	Value of meld
Minus score	15 points
0 to 1495	50 points
1500 to 2995	90 points
3000 to 6995	120 points
7000 or more	150 points

Wild cards

From three to seven wild cards (deuces and jokers) can be used to make a meld. A canasta of wild cards (seven cards) is called a Bolivia.

A Bolivia

2500 points

Sequence melds

Three or more cards forming a run of the same suit can be used to make a sequence meld. Suits rank from ace (high) to 4 (low); 3s and deuces cannot be included. Sequence melds can be natural or mixed with wild cards and score as normal. An Escalera is a natural sequence canasta (a run of seven cards of the same suit with no wild cards).

Mixed sequence canasta   300 points

An Escalera   1500 points

Going out

Two canastas are required to go out, one of which must be an Escalera.

Additional scoring

A Bolivia (wild canasta) scores 2500 points.

An Escalera (natural sequence canasta) scores 1500 points.

Red 3s count 100 points; all six score 1000.

Red 3 scores are plus when any two canastas have been made. If not, red 3 scores are minus.

Black 3s in melds count 5 points but left in the hand they count minus 100 points.

PENNIES FROM HEAVEN

Six people play in two partnerships of three, with a deck of 216 cards – i.e., 4 x 52 plus 8 jokers. Players sit in order A B A B A B around the table.

Dealing

Each player is dealt 13 cards singly, and finally a packet of 11 cards which remain face down until he has made his first canasta. He may then choose to add the packet of 11 cards to his hand.

A sample hand dealt for Pennies from Heaven

13 cards

11 cards

Playing

Two cards are taken from the stock and one discarded at each turn. Canastas may not include more than seven cards.

If a player wants to go out, his side must have made four canastas: one natural, one mixed, one wild and one of 7s.

The discard may not be a 7 until both sides have melded a canasta of 7s, whether mixed or natural; both types score 1500 points. A 7 may not be used when discarding to go out.

A natural canasta of 7s

Wild cards (jokers and deuces) can be melded; a canasta of wild cards scores 1000 points.

Scoring

Red 3s score 100 points each to the side, and 1000 points if all eight are held by one side. Red 3s only count as plus scores when a canasta of 7s has been made; otherwise they count minus.

The value of the opening meld

Score of side	Value of meld
Minus	15 points
0 to 495	50 points
500 to 995	90 points
1000 to 1495	120 points
1500 or more	150 points

The game is won by the side first reaching a score of 20,000 points.

MEXICANA

A partnership game for four players. A triple deck of 162 cards is used – i.e., 3 x 52 plus 6 jokers. Everyone is dealt 13 cards.

Playing

The player who makes the starting meld for his side draws 13 cards from the top of the stock to add to his hand.

When a 7 is on top, the discard pile cannot be taken. Sevens are melded as in standard canasta, but both mixed and natural canastas of 7s score 1000 points.

Going out

A partnership going out must have made two canastas and hold as many red 3s as it has made canastas.

Red 3s to go out in Mexicana

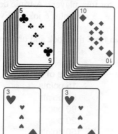

2 canastas need two red 3s

5 canastas need five red 3s

SAMBA

A partnership game for four players. A triple deck of 162 cards is used – i.e., 3 x 52 plus 6 jokers. Everyone is dealt 15 cards.

Two cards are drawn from the stock and one discarded at each turn.

The starting meld

Score of side	Value of meld
Minus	15 points
0 to 1495	50 points
1500 to 2995	90 points
3000 to 6995	120 points
7000 or more	150 points

Sequence melds

Sequence melds and canastas may be made by using three to seven cards of the same suit, running in rank order sequence (ace high to 4 low). A sequence canasta (seven cards) is called a samba and scores 1500 points.

No wild cards may be used and no further cards can be added to a samba.

Normal melds

No more than two wild cards may be used to make a mixed canasta.

Partnerships can combine their melds to make canastas or sambas.

The discard pile

The top card of the discard may not be added to a completed canasta, only to a meld of fewer than seven cards. The discard pile may only be taken by melding its top card with a natural pair from the hand.

Going out

To go out a partnership must have two canastas, two sambas or one of each.

Red 3s are only counted by the partnership going out: 100 each and 1000 for holding all six.

The bonus for going out is 200 points, but there is no extra bonus for going out concealed.

Winning the game

The winning side is credited the difference between their opponent's score and their own. Scores should therefore be checked after each deal to see if the difference would take one partnership up to the winning score of 10,000 points.

Calculating the scores

partnership A score:	5600 points
partnership B score:	3400 points
difference:	2200
add higher score:	5600
total:	7800 (insufficient to win game)

Later in the game:

partnership A score:	6950 points
partnership B score:	3810 points
difference:	3140
add higher score:	6950
total:	10,090 points

(partnership A wins the game)

COMBO-CANASTA

A high-scoring partnership game for four players. A triple deck of 162 cards is used – i.e., 3 x 52 plus 6 jokers. Everyone is dealt 15 cards.

Playing

Two cards are taken from the stock pile and one discarded. The discard pile is always frozen, so may only be taken if two natural cards are held that match the upcard.

In each deal, the first player to make a canasta gets a bonus of 11 cards from the stock.

There is no going out. The play for a deal ends when the stock is exhausted and any remaining discard is refused. A game consists of four deals.

Values of opening melds

Score of side	Value of first meld
0 to 3495	60 points
3500 to 6995	100 points
7000 to 10,495	140 points
10,500 and over	180 points

Melds and canastas

Only two wild cards can be used in mixed canastas. Wild cards may be melded by themselves in sequences of three or more runs. Canastas score as shown in the table.

Table of canasta scores

Bolivia (wild cards)	2000
Escalera (sequence)	1500
Samba (natural 7s)	1500
Mixed 7s	1000
Red canasta (natural)	500
Black canasta (mixed)	300

Red 3s score positive if the partnership has made a Bolivia, an Escalera or a Samba. If not, red 3s count as minus scores.

Scoring

At the end of four deals, each partnership deducts the value of cards left in the hand from the value of melds, canastas and red 3s, providing the required canastas have been made. The partnership with the higher score wins the game.

Points value of individual cards

Cards	Value	Penalty value
Jokers	50	-50
Deuces	20	-20
Aces	20	-20
K, Q, J, 10, 9, 8	10	-10
6,5,4	5	-5
7s	5	-500
black 3s	5	-200
red 3s	100	-100
six red 3s	2000	-2000
undeclared red 3		-500

Values of individual cards

+50 points each
-50 penalty

+20 points each

-20 penalty

+5 points each
-5 penalty

+10 points each
-10 penalty

+5 points each
-500 penalty

+2000 for all 6
-2000 penalty

+100 points each
-100 penalty
-500 if undeclared

+5 points each
-200 penalty

Canastas in combo-canasta

Bolivia (Wild)
2000 points

Escalera (Sequence)
1500 points

Samba (7s)
1500 points

Mixed 7s
1000 points

Red canasta (natural)
500 points

Black canasta (mixed)
300 points

Casino

Originating in 15th century France, this gambling game, while relatively easy to learn, requires skill with numbers.

Players

Two, three or four people can play.

Cards

The standard deck of 52 cards is used, the ace ranking low at a face value of 1. All other cards count at face value. Court cards have no numerical denomination.

Aim

Individuals score by capturing certain cards.

Dealing

The player making the lowest cut becomes the dealer.

Two players: the non-dealer gets two cards face down, two cards are placed face up on the table and two are dealt face down to the dealer. This is repeated until both players have a hand of four cards and four are face up on the table.

Three or four players: two cards are dealt face down to every player, including the dealer, then two face up on the table. This process is repeated once more.

Playing

The player to the dealer's left begins by playing at least one card to 'capture', 'build' or 'trail' cards. The others then play in turn by clockwise rotation.

Four ways of capturing cards

a) A pair can be made by capturing a face-up card with the same numerical value as a card in the hand. The player puts his card face down on the captured card and pulls them towards him.

Two or more face-up cards can be captured if a player holds a card to match each of them in value.

b) A group can be made by capturing two or more cards totalling the numerical value of a card in the hand.

c) A group and a pair can be made by capturing a group of two or three cards with the same value as one of the player's cards as well as a single card with the same value. A sweep is the capture of all four face-up cards in one turn.

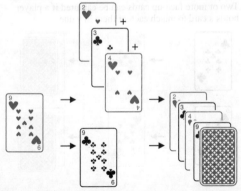

d) Court cards can be captured by making a pair or a group of all four, providing a matching court card is held. A group cannot be made with only three court cards.

Two ways of building

Face-up cards can be built on by adding cards from the hand. The purpose of building is to make it possible to capture cards. Court cards cannot be used in builds.

1) A player can make a single build by placing a card from his hand face up onto one of the face-up cards if:

a) the total value of the cards is not greater than 10; and

b) he holds, and declares, a card equal in value to his single build.

For example, a player holding a 7 and a 4 may build the 4 on a face up 3 and declare 'building 7'.

Building 7

Subsequently another player holding an ace and an 8 may, in turn, build the ace onto the 3+4 and declare 'building 8'. Cards being built remain in the centre of the table.

Building 8

2) A player may also change an existing single build into a multiple build. This is done by increasing the value of an existing single build and then using other cards to add another build of the same value, placing it at the side of the first build.

For example, a multiple build of 9 could be made on an existing single build of 5 by a player who holds a 4, plus 4, 5 and 9. He would declare 'building 9s'. His aim is use his 9 to capture all the cards in his next turn, hoping that nobody else captures it first.

Once the value of a multiple build has been established it cannot be changed.

A multiple build of 9

in hand

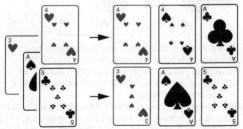

When a player has made or added to a build, in his next turn he must:

a) capture the build; or

b) add to a build; or

c) make a new build.

He is only exempt from these obligations if an opponent captures or builds before him.

Trailing

A player who cannot capture or build then trails by adding one card from his hand to the face-up cards on the table.

Renewing the hand

When all players have no cards left they are dealt another four cards each in packets of two, but no more are dealt to the centre of the table. New face-up cards can only come from a player who trails.

Completing a round

When the pack runs out, any cards remaining face up are claimed by the player who made the last capture. For each new round, players take the deal in turn. Six rounds complete a game.

Scoring

Only captured cards score points, as follows:

2 of spades (little casino):	1
10 of diamonds (big casino):	2
Each ace:	1
Seven or more spades:	1
27 or more cards:	3
A sweep:	1

Winning the game

The winner is the player who gets the highest score in one round, or 21 points over several rounds.

CASINO VARIATIONS
ROYAL CASINO

Court cards are given numerical values and can be
captured and used to build. The court cards count:

Js:	11
Qs:	12
Ks:	13

Aces may remain as 1 or may count as 14.

DRAW CASINO

Only the first 12 cards are dealt (for two players); after
that players draw from the stock to replenish cards in
their hands.

SPADE CASINO

Identical to the basic game but with additional scoring
for certain spades:

Ace of spades:	2
J of spades:	2
2 of spades:	2
Other spades:	1

The game is won by the player first gaining 61 points.

Cribbage

Thought to have been developed by Sir John Suckling, a poet and member of the English court in the early 17th century, cribbage requires a quick mind.

Players

The most popular game is six-card cribbage for two players. There are variations for three or four players as well.

Cards

A standard 52-card deck is used, all cards having their face value (ace is 1) and court cards counting 10.

The cribbage board

Although pencil and paper can be used for scoring, a cribbage board is much simpler. Usually a block of wood 10in by 3in, the board has four rows of 30 holes, in six groups of five pairs, two rows per player. At each end of the board are one or two game holes where the players keep their scoring pegs.

Moving the pegs to score

Each player uses two pegs, moving them alternately, first along the outer row and then along the inner.

a) The first score is marked by moving a peg the same number of holes along the outer row of holes.

b) The second score is marked by using a second peg to mark out the same number of holes beyond the first peg.

c) The third score is marked by using the first peg to count that score beyond the second peg.

d) To mark the next score, the peg that is behind is used to mark the score onwards from the front peg.

Scoring continues until the front peg reaches the game hole by passing the end of the inner row.

Cribbage board

Scoring with pegs

SIX-CARD CRIBBAGE (for two players)

Aim

The first player to go twice round the board, getting 121 points, wins the game.

Dealing

Players cut the deck and the one with the lower cut is first dealer. He deals six cards, face down and one at a time, to each player, beginning with his opponent. The rest of the deck is put aside.

The crib

Each player then discards two cards and places them face down to the right of the dealer to form the crib. The dealer will claim it as part of his score.

The cut

After the crib has been made, the non-dealer cuts the remaining deck. The top card is turned over by the dealer and left face up on the pack to be the start or starter. If this card is a J, two points 'for his heels' are scored by the dealer.

Scoring

Points can be scored for groups of cards made during play and when the hand is shown at the end. The following groups of cards score points:

a) Pair (two cards of the same rank): 2

b) Pair royal (three of the same rank): 6

c) Double pair royal (all four cards of the same rank): 12

d) Run (a sequence of cards in rank order): 1 point per card of any suit

e) Flush (any four or five cards of the same suit): 1 point per card

If also a run, it scores for both flush and run.

f) Fifteen (any group of cards with a total face value of 15): 2

Scoring

Playing

The non-dealer places one card from his hand face up in front of him and calls out its numerical value. The dealer then does the same.

The players continue to call as they add a card to their own spread of cards in turn, scoring for a pair, pair royal, run or fifteen they make with their opponent's card during play. Flushes are not taken into account during play.

Examples of some calls

Player	Card	Call	Score
Non-dealer	ace	'one'	0
Dealer	2	'run for two' (ace, 1)	2
Non-dealer	4	'four'	0
Dealer	5	'run for two'	2
Non-dealer	3	'fifteen for seven'	7

The non-dealer makes seven points from a fifteen: 1+2+4+5+3=15 (two points) plus a run: ace, 2, 4, 5, 3 (five points). Cards in a run do not have to have been played in the correct order.

The count

The face value of the cards is totalled as play proceeds. A sample count is shown for six cards played alternately by non-dealer and dealer.

Sample count

ace clubs	1
ace hearts	1
4 spades	4
5 clubs	5
10 diamonds	10
J clubs	10

The face values add up to 31, the limit for the count.

The player whose card reaches a count of 31 scores two extra points and both players' face-up cards are turned face down.

A player who cannot keep the count within 31 at his turn must call 'go'.

The opponent then plays any card low enough to keep the total below 31. If the count then reaches 31, he gets two points; if it is still less than 31, he gets one point and calls 'go'.

Play begins again, but with only the cards remaining in the hands, and continues until the count reaches 31 or all cards have been played. The player of the last card of a hand gains 'one for the last'.

The show

When all four cards of the hand have been played, the non-dealer begins the show by picking up his cards and showing the scores he can make with them.

If the non-dealer is close to reaching the winning score of 121, being the first to show can be an advantage. He then organises his cards in any combination for scoring (see Scoring **a** to **f**.) Both players can include the start card in their show. For example, if the start card is 4 hearts and a player has 4 clubs, 5 hearts, 6 clubs and 6 spades, the scoring combinations of 4, 4, 5, 6, 6 are:

8 points for fifteen (four combinations of 4, 5, 6);

12 points for runs (four runs of 4, 5, 6); and

4 points for pairs (5, 5, and 6, 6);

making a total of 24 points.

Sample show of 24 points

start card   cards from hand

Scoring combinations

8 points for fifteen
and 12 points for runs

4 points for pairs

Scoring cards of the same suit

A player holding a J of the same suit as the start card scores 'one for his nob'.

A player holding a flush of four cards of the same suit scores four points, but a four-card flush cannot be made with the start card. However, the start card can be added to make a flush of five, scoring five points. When the non-dealer has finished scoring his cards, the dealer does the same with first his own cards and then with the cards in the crib. The crib is scored like a hand, but only a five-card flush is counted. The dealer adds the crib score to his own.

Five-card flush in hearts

start card   cards in hand

Conventions

A redeal is required if there are errors in dealing. If a dealing mistake is found after play has begun, the non-dealer gains two points and the cards are redealt or extra cards are drawn from the stock pile.

If a player does not play his extra cards after a call of 'go', he may not play those cards later and his opponent gains two points. There are no penalties for counting errors during play.

A player scores an extra game in his favour if he reaches a score of 121 before his opponent is halfway round the board – i.e., before he reaches 61. This is called a 'lurch'.

In a rule not always used, a player may call his opponent 'muggins' when he has missed a score he could have made. The player can then add the missed score to his own.

FIVE-CARD CRIBBAGE

The rules are as for six-card cribbage with the following exceptions:

1) the aim is to win a game of 61 points;

2) five cards are dealt to each player; and

3) to compensate for not having the crib, the non-dealer pegs three points at the beginning.

SEVEN-CARD CRIBBAGE

Seven cards are dealt to each player and 181 points wins the game. Otherwise the rules are as for six-card cribbage.

THREE-HANDED CRIBBAGE

Five cards are dealt to each player, only one of which goes to the crib. The game is 61 points and there is no 31-point limit. The player to the left of the dealer both leads play and has the first show. Otherwise the rules are as for basic six-card cribbage.

FOUR-HANDED CRIBBAGE

This is the basic six-card game for partners, who sit opposite each other and play against the other partnership. The deal is usually five cards to each player, of which only one goes to the crib.

Ecarté

Meaning 'discarded', ecarté was popular in 19th-century France. Derivations of the game are the USA version called euchre and the three-handed game of five-hundred.

Players

Two people play against each other.

Cards

All cards below 7 are removed from a standard 52-card deck to make a deck of 32. The rank from high to low is K, Q, J, A, 10, 9, 8, 7. Two cards make a trick.

Rank

high   low

Aim

To score points by making tricks.

Preparing

Paper and pencil are needed for keeping the scores. Using the ranking of the 32-card deck, players cut for seat position, first deal and choice of deal for the whole game.

Dealing

The first dealer shuffles the cards and invites the non-dealer to cut. He deals five cards face down to his opponent and to himself, in packets of three then two or in packets of two then three.

The dealer places the eleventh card face up on the table
to assign trumps. If it is a K, the dealer gains one point.
The remaining cards are piled face down to form a stock.
If the non-dealer holds the king of trumps, he can gain a
point if he chooses to declare it.

The deal

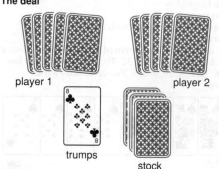

player 1

player 2

trumps

stock

The exchange

An exchange of cards can take place before play
commences but only if the non-dealer proposes one and
the dealer accepts.

To exchange, the non-dealer discards cards face down,
which are then dead, and takes the same number of
replacement cards from the stock. The dealer can then
make an exchange. This process continues until stopped
by the dealer declaring 'play' or until the stock pile runs
out, when play must start.

An exchange cannot be proposed by the dealer but he
can continue to exchange after the non-dealer signals he

does not wish to exchange by calling 'I play'.

An exchange should not be proposed or accepted if a player holds cards with which at least three tricks could be made.

Playing

The non-dealer leads with one card face up. The dealer must play a card of the same suit if he holds one. If not, his next option is a trump card; failing both, he can play any other card.

Tricks are won by the card of the leading suit that is higher in rank or by a trump card.

If trumps are led, only a higher ranking trump wins the trick.

The player winning a trick leads the next and so on until all five tricks are complete.

Scoring

There are four ways of gaining points:

a) Three tricks gains one point.

b) Five tricks, called a 'vole', gains two points.

c) King of trumps gains one point for the dealer if turned up immediately after the deal (see Dealing) or for a player who holds it if he declared it before playing his first card.

d) One point is gained if an opponent fails to make three tricks after refusing an exchange.

Five points wins the game.

Euchre

Originally one of the most popular trump games in the
USA, euchre, which derives from ecarté, probably
arrived in Louisiana with the French settlers.

Players

Four people play in pairs, partners sitting opposite each
other.

Cards

Every card below 7 is removed from a standard deck of
52 cards to make a 32-card deck in which ace ranks
high unless the suit is trumps.

In a trump suit the J from the suit of the same colour is
included and the ranking order from high to low is J
trumps, J suit of same colour, A trumps, K trumps, Q
trumps, 10, 9, 8 and 7 trumps.

Rank order when clubs is an ordinary suit

Rank order when clubs is trumps

Aim

Partners cooperate to win tricks.

Preparing

Each partnership takes the 3 and 4 of one suit from the stripped cards to use as score cards.

The lowest cut of the deck decides who deals. The dealer shuffles and offers the cut to the player on his left.

The players should agree at this stage whether they are going to play for a five-, seven- or ten-point game.

Dealing

Beginning on the dealer's left, cards are dealt face down in packets of three cards to each player on the first round and packets of two on the second round.

The next card, known as the upcard, is placed face up on the table to assign trumps. The remainder are placed faced down to form a stock.

Bidding for trumps

Starting with the player to the dealer's left, every player can bid to accept or reject the upcard as trumps.

In the first round, the dealer's opponents can accept by saying 'I order it up', his partner by saying 'I assist' and the dealer can accept by discarding one card from his hand and replacing it with the upcard.

If one player accepts the upcard, play begins.

Alternatively, the upcard can be rejected by non-dealers saying 'I pass' and by the dealer placing the card face up and visible under the stock.

If all players reject the upcard, a second round of bidding allows each player to either pass or nominate a different suit as trumps. The first nomination becomes the trump suit, and play begins.

If all players pass in the second round, cards are
shuffled and redealt by the next player in turn
clockwise.

The player who accepted the trump suit in the first
round or who nominated it in the second can choose to
play solo by declaring 'I play alone'.

His partner places his cards face down and takes no
further part in that round, although it is still the
partnership that scores points.

Playing

The player to the left of the dealer leads with one card
face up. Players must then play cards of the same suit.
If they cannot follow suit, they play either a trump card
or any other suit.

The player of the highest ranking card wins the trick
and leads for the next trick.

Scoring

The following points can be gained:

a) March (all five tricks): 2 points

b) March for a solo player: 4 points

c) Three or four tricks: 1 point

d) Euchred opponents – i.e., if they have made fewer
than three tricks: 2 points

The partners keep their scores by using the two cards
from the stripped pack as follows:

a) 1 point: place the 3 with the other across it

b) 2 points: place the 4 with the other across it

c) 3 points: place the 3 on top of the other card

d) 4 points: place the 4 on top of the other card

Scoring for higher scores is best done on paper.

Keeping the scores

Winning the game

Five, seven or ten points wins the game, as agreed at
the start.

EUCHRE VARIATIONS
RAILROAD EUCHRE

A version of four-handed euchre in which the joker is
also a trump and ranks over the right bower.

TWO-HANDED EUCHRE

Played as four-handed euchre, except the declaration to
play alone is not needed. A 24-card deck is used by
stripping the 7s and 8s from the 32-card deck.

THREE-HANDED EUCHRE

In the three-handed game, also known as cut-throat
euchre, the maker always plays alone against the other
two players in partnership. Scoring is the same except
that the maker only scores three points for a march, not
four.

CALL-ACE EUCHRE

A variation for four to six players, each playing alone,
with rules as in the four-handed game except for the
following:

Calling

The maker can opt to play alone or with a partner. To nominate a partner, he says 'I call on the ace of ...' and chooses a suit. The person holding the ace plays in partnership with the maker without declaring so until actually playing the ace. If the ace has not been dealt, the maker must play alone.

Scoring

When the maker plays alone he scores as follows:

a) for a march, as many points as there are players;

b) for three or four tricks, one point.

When the maker plays in partnership they score:

c) for a march, two points per player for three or four players, three points per player for five or six.

If the maker is euchred, whether alone or in partnership, all other players gain two points each.

Five hundred

A member of the euchre family, five hundred shares similarities with whist and bridge.

Players

The basic game is for three players; it can be played by two or four players, as well.

Cards

All cards below 7 are stripped from a standard 52-card deck and a joker is added to make a 33-card deck.

The rank order of the trump suit from high to low is joker, J trumps (known as right bower), J of same colour suit (left bower), ace, K, Q, 10, 9, 8 and 7 of trumps.

The rank order in no-trump hands is ace, K, Q, J, 10, 9, 8 and 7; there are no bowers. The joker becomes whatever suit is chosen by the person who holds it, and it ranks highest in that suit, taking any trick in which it is played.

A trick is a group of three cards, one played by each person in turn.

Rank order when spades are trumps

high   low

right left
bower bower

Rank order of all suits when there are no trumps

(Joker is nominated as clubs in this example.)

high   low

Aim

Individuals bid to make a contract and attempt to win by fulfilling it.

Dealing

The cards are cut for the deal. K ranks highest, joker lowest and ace next to lowest. The lowest cut determines the dealer.

Beginning with the player to the dealer's left, 10 cards are dealt to each player, face down in packets. The dealer can choose between: packets of three, two, three and two or packets of three, three, three and one.

The three cards left are called the widow and are placed in a pile face up on the table.

If there is any misdeal, the cards are thrown in and redealt by the next person in clockwise rotation.

Bidding

The player on the dealer's left begins by bidding the number of tricks he expects to make and stating his choice of trumps. Players must bid to make at least six tricks and not more than 10.

Each player bids in turn, clockwise, or passes. A pass prevents the player from making any further bid in that round.

Bids are ranked, from high to low: no-trumps, hearts, diamonds, clubs, spades. It can be seen from the scoring table that the most valuable contract is '10 no trumps' – i.e., 10 tricks without any trump suit, worth 520 points. The least valuable contract is 'six spades' – i.e., six tricks with spades as trumps, worth 40 points.

The player who makes the highest bid wins the contract and takes the widow cards. He then discards face down any three cards from his hand.

Playing

The player winning the contract is opposed by the other two who play as a partnership, although they each score for their own tricks.

The contract winner leads by placing one card face up on the table. The others follow suit, clockwise. Anyone who cannot follow the leading suit may play a card from another suit.

The winner of the trick is the person playing:

a) the highest card of the leading suit; or

b) the highest trump card, if the contract was for no-trumps; or

c) the joker.

The player winning the trick leads to the next one.

Scoring

If the winning bidder has fulfilled his contract, he scores as shown on the table. If not, he loses points to the value of the contract and his score may be a minus figure.

The opponents each score 10 points for each of their own tricks.

Scoring table for five hundred (values of contracts)

Tricks bid	♠	♣	♦	♥	No trumps
6	40	60	80	100	120
7	140	160	180	200	220
8	240	260	280	300	320
9	340	360	380	400	420
10	440	460	480	500	520

Bonus points

When a player who contracted to make eight or fewer tricks makes a grand slam (takes all 10 tricks), he gains 250 points. There are no other bonus points for making more tricks than contracted.

An optional bonus for a grand slam made by a player who contracted to make eight or more tricks is to double the value of the contract.

Winning the game

A score of 500 points wins the game. If two players both reach 500 in the same deal, the one who reached it first is the winner.

FIVE HUNDRED VARIATIONS

FIVE HUNDRED FOR TWO PLAYERS

This is dealt and played in the same way as the basic three-handed game except that the third hand becomes the 'dead hand'. It is left face down, bringing an element of chance to the players' bidding.

FIVE HUNDRED FOR FOUR PLAYERS

Partners sit opposite each other. The deck is increased by adding the 5s, 6s and two 4s, one black and one red, making a deck of 43. The bidding and play are as for the basic game. The winning bidder and his partner play to win against the other partnership.

Forty-five

This game is similar to loo and spoil five.

Players

Two, four or six people play in teams, one against one, two against two or three against three.

Cards

The standard 52-card deck is used but has a very unusual ranking in both plain (non-trump) suits and trump suits. The ranking, from high to low, is as follows.

Clubs and spades

As plain suits: K, Q, J, ace, 2, 3, 4, 5, 6, 7, 8, 9, 10.

As trump suits: 5, J, ace hearts, ace, K, Q, 2, 3, 4, 6, 7, 8, 9, 10.

Diamonds

As plain suit: K, Q, J, 10, 9, 8, 7, 6, 5, 4, 3, 2, ace.

As trump suit: 5, J, ace hearts, ace, K, Q, 10, 9, 8, 7, 6, 4, 3, 2.

Hearts

As plain suit: K, Q, J, 10, 9, 8, 7, 6, 5, 4, 3, 2.

As trump suit: 5, J, ace, K, Q, 10, 9, 8, 7, 6, 4, 3, 2.

Rank in plain suits

Clubs and spades

high　　　　　　　　　　　　　　　　　　　　　　low

Diamonds

high   low

Hearts

high   low

Rank in trump suits
Clubs and spades

high   low

Diamonds

high   low

Hearts

high   low

A trick is a group of two, four or six cards, one played by each person in turn.

Aim

Teams try to win tricks and to stop the opposition from making them.

Preparing

There are two scoring systems (see Scoring) so players should agree beforehand which system to use.

Dealing

Players draw a card for the deal, with the cards ranking as normal (ace high and 2 low). The dealer is the player who draws the lowest card.

A packet of two, then a packet of three cards are dealt face down to each player in turn clockwise. When everyone has five cards, the next card is turned face up to indicate trumps for that hand.

The exchange

Exchanging relates to the ace of the trump suit and only to the ace of hearts when hearts is the trump suit.

If the trump indicator card is the ace, the dealer may take it and replace it with a card from his hand.

If it is not the ace, a player who holds the ace of trumps may declare he is holding it and exchange the face-up card for any card in his hand.

If he chooses not to make an exchange, he must declare he is holding the ace at his first turn; otherwise the ace is devalued and becomes the lowest ranking trump card.

Playing

The player to the left of the dealer leads with one card face up. The others play a card in turn until a trick is completed.

If the leading card is a plain suit, players may follow suit or use a trump. If neither is possible, a card from another plain suit may be played.

If the leading card is a trump suit, players usually must follow suit if they can, unless one of the top three trumps – i.e., the 5 and J of trumps and the ace of hearts – is held.

The hand continues until all cards have been played to tricks. The winner of a trick leads to the next.

Scoring

Points for each hand are scored only by the team making the most tricks in that hand.

There are two scoring systems:

1) making three or four tricks gives a score of 5 points; five or more tricks a score of 10 points;

2) making three tricks gives a score of 5 points, four tricks a score of 15 points and five or more a score of 25 points.

The first team to reach a score of 45 is the winner.

Grand

In this game, the winning bidder chooses which of four similar games shall be played: whist, euchre, hearts or grand.

Players

Four people play in pairs. The game is not suitable for other numbers of players.

Cards

The standard 52-card deck is used. It is ranked and may be stripped according to which game is chosen.

A trick is a set of four cards, one from each player in turn.

Rank for whist (52-card deck), plain and trumps

high   low

Rank for euchre (32-card deck), plain suits

high   low

Rank for euchre trump suit, when clubs are trumps

J of   J of same
trumps   colour

high   low

Rank for hearts and grand (52-card deck), no trumps

high   low

Aim

Each pair attempts to make the highest bid and then
make enough tricks to fulfil it.

Preparing

Pencil and paper will be needed to keep the scores and
make the final calculations. Players should agree in
which of three ways the game will end (see Winning the
game).

Dealing

Players cut the cards and the highest card deals; ace
ranks low for the cut.

Beginning with the player to the left of the dealer, the
whole pack is dealt singly, face down in clockwise
rotation, until each player has 13 cards.

Bidding

In the same order as for the deal, each player then has one turn only to make a bid or pass. He bids the number of points he would expect to score as the highest bidder. The bid must be five or a multiple of five.

If the other three players pass, the dealer must make a bid.

The player making the highest or only bid then declares his choice of game for the hand: whist, euchre, hearts or grand.

Playing

The winning bidder always leads play with any card from his hand. He and his partner play to fulfil his bid and the other partnership attempts to prevent them. Otherwise, play follows the rules of the selected game with the conditions as listed for each option.

The whist option

The bids can be 5, 10, 15, 20, 25, 30 or 65. The bidder names the trump suit before he begins play.

Scoring the whist option

The first six tricks do not score points. After that, each trick scores 5 points. For example, if the bid is 20 points, the partnership must make 10 tricks (6 + 4 = 10). If all 13 tricks are won (a grand slam) then all tricks score, making a total of 65 points. There are no scores for honour cards (in whist these are ace, K, Q and J of trumps).

Setbacks

If the partnership fails to fulfil its bid, the points bid are deducted from its previous score. There may be a minus score. In this situation, the opposing partnership gains 5 bonus points for every trick made over six.

The grand option

Grand is the same as whist, but without trumps.

Scoring the grand option

The first six tricks make no score; the seventh and subsequent tricks score 9 points each.

A grand slam (all 13 tricks) scores an extra 40 points, making a total of 103. A partnership making a grand slam automatically wins that game.

Setbacks

If the partnership fails to fulfil its bid, the points bid are deducted from the team's previous score. When this happens, the opposing partnership gains nine bonus points for every trick it takes over six.

The euchre option

The high bidder can only choose euchre when bidding 25 or less. The trump suit is declared by the bidder. Then each player discards any eight cards face down, including trump cards below an 8. The size of the bid determines how the bidder plays: if he bid lower than 20 he must play in partnership; if he bid 20 he chooses to play in partnership or alone; if he bid 25 he must play alone.

When playing alone, the bidder may ask for his partner's best card in exchange for one of his own. His partner then leaves his cards face down on the table. Play then proceeds as for euchre.

Scoring the euchre option

Three tricks score 5 points; four tricks score 10 points; five tricks score 20 points when made by partners and 25 points when made alone.

Setbacks

If a bid is not fulfilled, the partnership deducts the

points bid plus 20 points from its previous score. The
lone player's penalty is twice the number of points bid.
There is no bonus to the opposition.

The hearts option

Play is as for the game of hearts. This option can only
be chosen when the bid is 50 or less.

Scoring the hearts option

Bidding partners win 50 points if they avoid making
any tricks in hearts.

Setbacks

For every trick containing a heart made by the bidders,
the penalty is the amount bid plus 1 point for each heart
card used. Their opponents lose 1 point for every heart
card they use.

Convention of the heart bid option

When the dealer's partnership has a score of less than
70, it is assumed that if the first bidder passes, he is
prepared to play the game of hearts. When the dealer's
partnership score is 70 or more, the first bidder can
ensure hearts are played by declaring hearts and
leading with a heart card.

Winning the game

There are three ways a game may end:
1) when one partnership has scored 100 points;
2) when a fixed time limit has been reached; or
3) when a fixed number of rounds have been played.
The final result is calculated from the scores held by
the two partnerships at the end of the game:
1) the lower score is deducted from 100 and assigned
to the partnership with the higher score; and
2) the number of setbacks for each partnership is
recorded. The difference between them is multiplied by

10 and assigned to the partnership with fewer setbacks.
The winner is the partnership with the higher score
from these calculations.

Sample calculation

	Score	Number of setbacks
Side A	70	8
Side B	60	5

1) 100 - 60 = 40 assigned to A.
2) (8 - 5) x 10 = 30 assigned to B.

The winner of the game is partnership A with a final
score of 40, beating B's 30.

Hearts

A 19th-century game in which players try to avoid
taking penalty cards.

Players

Any number from three to seven people, each playing
for themselves.

Cards

The standard 52-card deck is used. Ace ranks high and
there are no trump cards. The 2s are stripped from the
deck according to the number of players. The 2 of
hearts is always retained.

One card played by each person in turn makes a trick.

Table of numbers

Players	Stripped cards	Cards in a trick
Three	One 2	3
Four	None	4
Five	Two 2s	5
Six	Three 2s	6
Seven	Three 2s	7

Rank

Aim

Players make tricks and score penalty points for every hearts card they use. Thus the aim is to score zero by avoiding the use of heart cards in tricks.

Preparing

Paper and pencil will be needed for scoring penalty points. Players should agree beforehand how the game is to be won. The options are:

1) the game ends when one person reaches a penalty score of 50 points; or

2) the game ends when an agreed number of rounds have been played, usually four or five.

Dealing

The player making the lowest cut becomes the dealer. Beginning with the player on his left, he deals the cards face down, singly, to each player in clockwise rotation, until all the cards are dealt.

Number of cards in each hand

Players	Deck	Hand
Three	51	17
Four	52	13
Five	50	10
Six	49	8 (The last card is put aside.)
Seven	49	7

Playing

The player on the left of the dealer leads the first trick by playing one card. The other players must follow suit if they can. If not, they may play any other card. The trick is claimed by the person playing the highest ranking card of the lead suit. That player leads the next trick.

The hand ends when all 13 heart cards have been played, unless a player fails to correct a revoke.

Revoking

If a player revokes – i.e., fails to follow suit when he could have – he may correct his mistake before the trick is claimed. Otherwise he scores 13 penalty points and the round ends immediately. No penalties are scored by the other players.

The deal for the next round passes clockwise to the player on the left of the last dealer.

Scoring

At the end of each round, every heart card in a player's tricks counts as one penalty point. Any cards left in the hand do not count.

Cards scoring one penalty point

Winning the game

The winner is the player with the lowest number of penalty points at the agreed stage of the game – i.e., after a player has scored 50 points or the agreed number of rounds has been played (see Preparing).

HEARTS VARIATIONS

These eight popular variations of hearts are all played the same as the basic game with differences as indicated.

SPOT HEARTS

A scoring variation, each heart card counts as its face value.

Spot hearts penalty points

Card	Penalty score
Ace	1
K	13
Q	12
J	11
10 to 2	face value

Penalty cards

1 13 12 11 10 9 8 7 6 5 4 3 2

BLACK LADY

The Q of spades is an extra penalty card valued at 13 points. A player with the Q of spades in his hand must use it as soon as possible. All hearts score one penalty point as in the basic game.

13 penalty points

GREEK HEARTS

After the first deal of a game, each player examines his hand and chooses three cards to pass, face down, to the player on his right. A player may only look at the cards he is receiving after he has passed his own cards. The Q of spades is used as an extra penalty card and penalty points are scored as shown.

Greek hearts penalty points

Q♠	K♥	Q♥	J♥	10♥	9♥	8♥	7♥	6♥	5♥	4♥	3♥	2♥	A♥
13	13	50	11	10	9	8	7	6	5	4	3	2	1

A player who takes tricks containing all 14 penalty cards makes a zero score. When this happens, all other players score 150 penalty points regardless of which cards they have played.

DOMINO HEARTS

Each player is dealt only six cards and the rest form a stock pile, face down.

Players draw a card from the stock when they cannot follow suit, and continue drawing until they can, keeping all the extra cards to use in play. When the stock is finished, players then discard, as in basic hearts.

As players use up their cards, they drop out. The last player left in then counts one penalty point for each heart card in both his tricks and his hand. The others all score one penalty point for heart cards in their tricks. The game ends when one player reaches a penalty score of 31. The winner is the player with the lowest score.

JOKER HEARTS

The 2 of hearts is removed from the deck and the joker is included, ranking below the J of hearts. All heart cards carry one penalty point each, as in the basic game of hearts. However, the joker scores five penalty points.

The joker wins any trick in which it is played, regardless of suit, except if a higher ranking heart card is played – i.e., J, Q , K or ace of hearts.

Rank for joker hearts

5
penalty
points

HEARTSETTE

A widow hand is placed face down on the table and remains there. The number of cards depends on the number of players, as shown in the table.

Cards in the widow

Players	Widow	Deck
Three	3	51 (2 of spades removed)
Four	3	51 (2 of spades removed)
Five	2	52
Six	4	52
Seven	3	52

After the widow has been dealt, all other cards are dealt among the players. The first person to make a trick also takes the widow and scores penalty points for any hearts in it.

HEARTS FOR TWO

Each player is dealt 13 cards; the rest form a stock. The winner of each trick takes the top card from the stock and the loser takes the next card.

The game ends when all cards have been played.
Scoring is as for basic hearts.

BLACK MARIA

The game (also called Slippery Anne) is the same as
basic hearts, but there are three extra cards carrying
high penalty points:

Black Maria, the Q of spades:	13 points
the K of spades:	10 points
the ace of spades:	7 points

An exchange of three cards from each player to the
person on his right takes place before play, as in Greek
hearts.

When all penalty cards have been played, the round
ends.

Penalty cards in Black Maria

13 points	10 points	7 points

1 point each

Imperial

A game for two players, similar to piquet.

Cards

Imperial requires a piquet deck of 32 cards, made by stripping 6s, 5s, 4s, 3s and 2s from a 52-card deck. The cards rank from high to low: K, Q, J, ace, 10, 9, 8, 7. The trump suit is declared for each hand. The K, Q, J, ace and 7 of trumps are the honour cards.

Cards count their face value; aces count 11 and court cards count 10 each.

Rank

high   low

Honours when clubs are trumps

high   low

A pool of chips is used for scoring

Chips

For each point scored, one white chip is taken. When a
player has six white chips, he trades them for one red.
When a player gains a red chip, his opponent loses all
his white chips back to the pool.

Aim

Players try to win five red chips from the pool by
scoring before, during and after play in each deal.

Dealing

Players cut for deal. The dealer shuffles and the non-
dealer cuts. Cards are dealt face down in four packets
of three, beginning with the non-dealer.

When both players have 12 cards, the next (25th) card
determines trumps for that deal and is placed face up.
The remaining cards are set aside.

Scoring before play

1) If the turned-up trump card is an honour card, the
dealer scores one white chip.

2) If a hand is carte blanche (contains no K, Q or J),
the player scores one white chip.

3) Combinations of cards are then declared and scored.

4) Combinations including the upcard are declared and
scored last of all.

Scores for combinations

Cards can be combined as 'points', sequences or melds
and are declared and scored in that order. A player can
use any card in his hand in more than one combination.

A point is the suit in which a player holds the greatest
number of cards. The player with the longer suit scores
the point and claims one white chip for each card.

In case of a draw, the player whose point has the higher

total face value scores. If there is still a draw, the non-dealer gains the score.

Sample scoring for points

Dealer's point   Non-dealer's point

point score:
5 white chips   5 white chips

result: a draw

value score:
7+8+10+11+10 = 46   7+10+10+10 +10 = 47
non-dealer wins points score of 5 white chips

A sequence is a run of three or four consecutive cards (the K, Q, J or ace only) of the same suit. Four cards beat three and the higher ranking card sequence wins one red chip. The non-dealer scores in a draw.

Sample sequences

dealer   non-dealer

K ranks higher than a Q so dealer wins one red chip for the best sequence

Melds are groups of cards of the same rank. In imperial, a combination of four Ks, four Qs, four Js, four aces or four 7s form a meld and rank in that order with K high. The best meld scores one red chip.

Sample melds

  dealer   non-dealer

Q ranks higher than J so non-dealer wins one red chip for the best meld

How to declare combinations

Combinations are declared formally, to avoid giving the opponent too much information.

The non-dealer begins in each of the three declarations: points, sequence and meld.

Point declaration

1) Non-dealer: 'A point of...' (states number).

2) Dealer has three possible replies:

a) 'Good' if he concedes.

b) 'Not good' if his point is longer. He then states the length of his point and the score he claims.

c) 'How many?' if his point is the same length.

3) If the dealer asked 'how many?' the non-dealer then states the face value of his point.

4) Dealer answers 'good' if he concedes; 'not good' if the face value of his point is larger; or 'equal' if the value of his point is the same. In this case, the non-dealer scores.

5) The winner then declares the length and face value of his point and claims the score.

Sample points declaration

dealer's point

value: 46

non-dealer's point

value: 47

Non-dealer: 'A point of five.'
Dealer: 'How many?'
Non-dealer: 'Value 47.'
Dealer: 'Good.'
Non-dealer: 'A point of five, value 47, I score five.'

Sequence declaration

The non-dealer begins by declaring: 'A sequence of....'
He states the number and the procedure continues as in points declaration.

Sample sequence declaration

dealer

non-dealer

Non-dealer: 'A sequence of three.'
Dealer: 'How high?'
Non-dealer: 'Queen.'
Dealer: 'Not good. King. I score one.'

Meld declaration

The non-dealer begins by declaring: 'Four...,' stating the suit of his meld. The procedure continues as before, with the dealer replying:

'Good' if he concedes;

'Not good' if he holds a meld of a higher ranking card or his meld trumps his opponent's; or

'Equal' if he has a meld of the same denomination.

Sample meld declaration

non-dealer   dealer

Non-dealer: 'Four aces.'

Dealer: 'Good.'

Non-dealer: 'Four aces. I score one.'

Adding point, sequence and meld scores

Each player adds the score for the previous declaration to the current one. Taking the samples given above, the accumulated scores would be declared as follows:

Non-dealer: 'A point of five.'

Dealer: 'How many?'

Non-dealer: 'Value 47.'

Dealer: 'Good.'

Non-dealer: 'A point of five, value 47, I score five. (pause) A sequence of three.'

Dealer: 'How high?'

Non-dealer: 'Queen.'

Dealer: 'Not good. King. I score one.'

Non-dealer: 'Four aces.'

Dealer: 'Good.'

Non-dealer: 'Four aces. I score five.' He then totals his score and says, 'I start with...,' stating his total, which will be 10 plus another 5 if he was dealt a carte blanche. The dealer ends up with no score because he must return his white chip to the pool when the non-dealer wins his second red chip.

Finally, sequence and melds using the upcard are declared and scored in the same manner.

Playing

The first trick is led by the non-dealer; each trick is then led by the winner of the previous one.

The second player must take the trick if possible and must follow suit if he can. If he can't, he must trump it. If he can do neither, he is allowed to discard.

Tricks remain face up on the table in front of the player who won them; he is free to examine them.

Scoring during play

One red chip is won:

1) by a player using a K or Q to take the J of trumps;

2) by a player taking the ace.

One white chip is won for every trump honour card included in the tricks a player wins.

Scoring at the end of play

The player with the most tricks wins one white chip for each trick in excess of his opponent's.

Two red chips are gained by gained by a player winning all 12 tricks, called the capot.

Winning the game

The game is won by the player who first gets five red chips. If this happens during play, the hand is abandoned.

Klaberjass

Very similar to the French championship game of
belotte, klaberjass – also known as kalabriasz,
Kolobiosh, klab or clobber – is an interesting game for
two players.

Cards

A 52-card deck is stripped of all 6s, 5s, 4s, 3s and 2s to
produce a 32-card deck. The ranking is unusual both in
plain and trump suits as shown. The 7 of trumps is
called the dix.

Ranking in all plain suits

high   low

Ranking when a suit is trumps

high   low
                                                   the dix

Aim

Each player tries to reach a score of 500 points by
melding sequences and taking tricks containing high
scoring cards.

Dealing

The first dealer is chosen by high cut using standard ranking with ace low. After the shuffle and cut, six cards are dealt face down to each player in two packets of three. The next card is turned up in the centre of the table and the remaining cards placed next to it, face down, as the stock.

Bidding for trumps

There are three ways of bidding:

1) 'Accept' means the suit of the central upcard is trumps.
2) 'Pass' means the bidding passes to the next player.
3) 'Schmeiss' means a new deal is proposed.

The non-dealer begins the bidding. If his bid is pass, it becomes the dealer's turn to bid.

If his bid is schmeiss, the dealer then has to choose between agreeing to a new deal or making a bid of accept. He may also pass, leading to a new round of bids.

If the dealer chooses to bid accept, the non-dealer then has to accept or pass. If he passes, the dealer then has a second bid.

If the dealer also passes in this second round, the bidding ends and there is a new deal.

The maker is the name given to the player who wins the bid by determining trumps.

The second deal

When trumps have been determined, three more cards are dealt to each player singly.

The bottom card is then taken from the stock and placed face up on top of the pile. A player who holds the dix (7 of trumps) may exchange it for this top card, providing trumps were determined by the acceptance of the central upcard.

Players then examine their cards to find which sequences they are holding.

Sequences

A sequence is a consecutive run of three or more cards of the same suit.

A three-card sequence scores 20 points.

A sequence of four or more scores 50 points.

The rank order for sequence building is ace, K, Q, J, 10, 9, 8, 7. When sequences are of the same value, they rank according to their highest value card. All trump cards outrank plain suit cards.

If two sequences in plain suits are still of equal value, neither player scores. Some people vary this rule and make the non-dealer's sequence the highest.

Sequences

20 points

50 points

Declaring sequences

This is usually done before play starts, but may be done after the non-dealer has started play by placing his lead card to the first trick. The declaration is to show which player holds the higher sequence.

The non-dealer starts by declaring:

a) 'sequence of 20' for a three-card sequence; or

b) 'sequence of 50' for one of four or more.

The dealer replies:

a) 'good' if he concedes;

b) 'not good' if he can declare a higher sequence; or

c) 'how high?' if he has a sequence of the same value.

In this case the non-dealer declares the highest ranking card of his sequence.

In reply the dealer declares 'good' or 'not good.'

Scoring the winning sequence

The player who has declared the highest sequence must then show it before claiming the score. He may also score for any other sequences he holds, providing he shows them. The other player gets no score at this stage.

Playing

The first trick is led by the non-dealer and the suit must be followed, trumped or a discard played, in that order. If the leading suit is trumps, it must be trumped if possible. The player winning the trick claims it and leads to the next trick.

Bella

A player who holds the K and Q of trumps is said to hold the bella. It is worth 20 points, but only when each card has been played to take a trick. If the player also holds the J of trumps, he scores for both the bella and the sequence.

Scoring during play

When a player takes one of the following cards in

The bella when clubs are trumps

tricks, he scores accordingly:

the jasz (J of trumps):   20 points
the menel (9 of trumps):   14 points
aces: 11 points
10s: 10 points
Ks: 4 points
Qs: 3 points
Js (except the jasz):   2 points

The last trick scores 10 points for the player taking it.

Scoring during play when spades are trumps

| Trumps | jasz
20 points | menel
14 points | 11 points |
| 10 points | 4 points | 3 points | plain suits
2 points |

Scoring the hand

After all nine tricks have been taken, the score for the
hand is made as follows:

1) If the maker (the player who won the trumps bid)
has the higher score, both players keep their own scores.

2) If the maker's opponent has the higher score, he

'goes bate' by scoring both his own and the maker's total.

3) If both players have the same points total, the maker 'goes half bate' by scoring nil, and his opponent keeps his own score.

Winning the game

The first player to reach 500 points wins the game.

If both players reach 500 points in the same hand, the one with the higher final score wins.

KLABERJASS VARIATIONS

THREE-HANDED KLABERJASS

The deal and play rotate clockwise around the table.

The maker must go bate or score more than the sum of his opponents' scores.

Sequences and points scored in play are kept individually, but if the maker goes bate, the opponents share his points.

FOUR-HANDED KLABERJASS

The deal and play proceed clockwise. Everyone is dealt eight cards, except the dealer who gets seven.

The player holding the dix trades it for the central up card, as in the standard game, but the dealer then takes the dix as the eighth card in his hand.

The partner of the player who has declared the highest sequence also scores his own sequences.

Partners combine their scores and keep their tricks together. The rules for winning the game are as for the standard game, the two partnerships scoring as if they were two players.

Knaves

A game for three players using a standard 52-card deck
with ace ranking high. Knaves is played like whist, but
Js in tricks taken count as minus points.

Rank

high   low

Aim

To score points for tricks taken, while avoiding
penalties for tricks with Js. A trick is a group of three
cards, one played by each person in turn.

Preparing

Paper and pencil are needed for scoring.

Dealing

The player making the highest cut becomes the first
dealer. The whole deck is dealt in clockwise direction,
beginning with the player on the dealer's left.
Cards are dealt singly and face down, except the last
card, which is turned up. The suit of this card is the
trump suit for the hand and the card is claimed by the
dealer at his first turn.
Players can agree to correct any misdeal unless anyone
claims a redeal.

Playing

The player to the left of the dealer leads with one card.
The other players follow suit in turn with one card. If a
player cannot follow suit, he may play any other card.
The trick is won by the highest trump card or the
highest card of the leading suit.

The winner claims the trick by turning it face down
near him and leading the next trick.

Play continues until 13 tricks have been made. The
cards are then shuffled and dealt by the next person in
clockwise direction from the first dealer.

Each person plays for himself, but two players may
form a temporary partnership in an attempt to reduce
the lead of the third player.

Scoring

One point is scored for each trick taken. Points are
deducted for tricks containing the following cards:

J of hearts:	4 points
J of diamonds:	3 points
J of clubs:	2 points
J of spades:	1 point

The final score could be positive or negative.

Winning the game

The first person to gain 20 positive points is the winner.

Penalty cards

-4 points   -3 points   -2 points   -1 points

POLIGNAC

A French game of knaves for four to six players, in which the J of spades is known as polignac. The aim is to avoid taking tricks containing Js, especially the polignac.

Cards

The standard 52-card deck is stripped of 2s, 3s, 4s, 5s and 6s when there are four players. If there are five or six players, the black 7s are also stripped.

Dealing and playing

The cards are dealt and played as for the standard game of knaves except there are no trumps. Before the start of a game, it is usual to agree how many hands shall make the game.

Rank for four players

Rank for five or six players

Scoring

Players score penalty points for any Js they have taken during the hand. The Js of hearts, diamonds and clubs each carry one penalty point. The polignac (J of spades) carries two penalty points.

General

If a player decides to take all the tricks in a hand, known as playing 'general', he must declare his intention before the leading card is played.

If he is successful, everyone else deducts five penalty points from their score.

If he is unsuccessful, he deducts five penalty points from his own score. Those who take the Js score penalties as usual.

Winning the game

The player with the fewest points after the agreed number of hands is the winner.

Penalty cards

-1 point each

polignac
-2 points

Loo

Once one of the most popular of European card games,
loo, also known as lanterloo, is played for stakes.

THREE-CARD LOO

A variation for three or more players, although six
players make it most interesting.

Cards

A standard deck of 52 cards is used, with ace ranking
high.

Rank

high   low

Aim

Everyone attempts to win at least one trick. There is a
penalty for failing to take any trick, known as being
'looed'. Before beginning the game, players should
agree whether to play 'limited loo' or 'unlimited loo'
(see looing).

Dealing

The player making the lowest cut shuffles and deals
three cards, singly and face down, to each player. He
also deals an extra hand, called a 'miss'. He may deal it
as the first or last hand of a round. The next card is
turned face up and indicates trumps.

The pool

Each player puts three counters into the pool. However, the dealer may choose to make the opening deal a 'single' by not dealing a miss. In this case only the dealer will put three counters into the pool.

In subsequent deals, the deal passes clockwise. The option to deal a single is only available on the opening deal.

The choice

Each player chooses one of the following, starting with the player on the left of the dealer:

a) To play with the cards he holds, saying 'I play'.

b) To throw in his hand and take the miss, saying 'I take the miss'.

c) To pass, saying 'I pass' as he throws in his cards, sitting out that deal. If everyone has passed, the dealer takes the pool.

When only one player has chosen to play and has taken the miss, the dealer has the option of either playing with him or letting him take the pool. If only one player chooses to play but does not take the miss, the dealer must play him using the miss cards. The dealer neither loses nor gains counters, regardless if he wins or loses.

Playing

The first person who chose to play leads with his highest trump, if he holds one. Other players who did not pass follow suit in turn, attempting to take the trick with a higher card. If any player cannot follow suit, he should play a trump if possible. As a last resort he may discard.

The player who wins the trick must lead, whenever possible, with a trump.

Scoring

One third of the pool is taken by each player who wins
a trick.

Looing

If a player does not take a trick, he is 'looed'. If limited
loo has been chosen, the penalty is to pay an agreed
number of counters into the pool, usually three. If
unlimited loo has been chosen, he must pay as many
counters as there were in the pool when the hand began.

Penalties

A player is also looed for the following:

a) examining the miss but not taking it;

b) not leading the ace of trumps when it is in his hand;

c) not taking a trick when he can; and

d) playing when it is not his turn.

Variations of the rules

The game is sometimes played so that the trump suit is
revealed only when a player cannot follow suit.

Another option is that if three trumps are dealt to one
player, that player takes the pool and the hands are
thrown in, shuffled and redealt.

FIVE-CARD LOO

Played as for three-card loo with a few different
conventions.

Dealing

Each player has five cards and no miss is dealt.

Pool

Players give five, not three, counters to the pool.

Exchanges

During the choice, a player may exchange his hand (or
part of it) for up to five cards from the stock, but must
then play his new hand.

Pam

The J of clubs is known as 'pam' and outranks all other cards, regardless of which is the trump suit.

A player leading the ace of trumps may say 'pam be civil'. Pam cannot be played to that trick.

Flushes

Five cards of the same suit, or four cards plus pam, are called a flush. Anyone holding a flush shows it before play and claims the pool. All other players then become looed unless they too hold a flush.

A flush of five trumps wins the pot and the hand over other flushes. If two flushes are equal, the one with the highest ranking card wins. If two or more players have equal plain suit flushes, they divide the pool equally.

Sample flushes

pam

Blaze

The blaze is a hand made entirely of court cards; it outranks a flush. A player dealt a blaze wins the pot and the hand. If two blazes are equal, the one with the highest ranking card wins.

Sample blazes

pam

Michigan

A fast-moving, challenging game for beginners and
experienced players alike. Michigan is played for
stakes by three to eight people. It is also known as
Boodle, Chicago, Newmarket or Saratoga.

Cards

A standard 52-card deck is used, with ace ranking high.
The J of spades, Q of diamonds, K of clubs and ace of
hearts from another pack form the 'boodle'. These four
cards are placed separately, face up, in the centre of the
table.

Boodle cards

Preparing

Players cut the cards for sitting positions, the one
drawing the highest card having first choice and the
others sitting clockwise in order of cut. Everyone
begins with the same number of counters or chips.
Players should decide how the game is to be won by
agreeing:

a) a time limit for the game;

b) how many deals shall be played; or

c) how many chips shall be the winning number.

Aim

Each player tries to gain chips by playing cards matching the boodle and by being the first to play all his cards.

Ante

Players ante by placing one chip on each boodle card before the deal for each hand.

Dealing

The player making the highest cut becomes the first dealer. Subsequent deals rotate clockwise.

The whole pack is dealt, singly and face down, starting with an extra hand to the dealer's left, known as the widow. All hands should have an equal number of cards, though the pack may not divide evenly due to the number of players.

The auction

Before play, the dealer can exchange his hand for the widow and discard his own hand face down.

If the dealer does not take the widow, the others may bid for it. The player making the highest bid pays chips to the dealer, takes the widow and discards his own hand face down.

If nobody bids for the widow, it remains face down.

Playing

The player to the dealer's left lays down his lowest card face up in front of him, announcing its rank and suit. Whoever holds the next higher card in the same suit plays it in the same way in front of himself. This may be the same player.

Cards continue to be played in sequence, by whichever player holds them, until the ace is played or nobody has the next card.

Each player has his own pile of face-up cards, but once he has covered a card, it cannot be examined again.

Stopping play

When a sequence ends, play is 'stopped' and the last player begins a new sequence with the lowest card he has in another suit. If he cannot do so, play passes to the next person sitting clockwise. If nobody can play, the original player may start a new sequence in the same suit as before.

Boodle winnings

If someone plays a card the same as a boodle card, he takes all the chips on that card. If nobody claims any of the boodle chips, they remain in place.

Before every new deal, each player antes a chip onto each boodle card.

End of play

When one player has used all his cards, play ends. The other players must then pay him one chip for every card they hold.

Penalty

When a card that should be is not played in sequence, that player pays one chip to each opponent. If his failure has prevented someone else from gaining boodle chips, he must use his own chips to make good the loss. The boodle chips remaining are carried over to the next hand.

Winning the game

As decided during preparation for play, the winner is either:

a) the first person to gain an agreed number of chips; or

b) the player holding the most chips after an agreed time or an agreed number of deals.

Napoleon

Similar to euchre, napoleon (or nap) is a game for two to seven people who each play alone for stakes, using counters.

Aim

The highest bidder attempts to fulfil his contract by taking tricks while the other players try to prevent him.

Cards

A standard deck of 52 cards is used, with ace ranking high.

Dealing

The player making the highest cut becomes the first dealer. Subsequent deals rotate clockwise.

Five cards are dealt, face down and singly, to each player. The remainder is placed face down to form the stock.

Rank

high   low

Bidding

The player to the left of the dealer begins the bidding. He can pass or bid to make two, three, four or five tricks. Five tricks is called a napoleon. Players bid in turn and must make a higher bid than the previous one. There is only one round of bidding, and the 'bidder' is the person who makes the highest bid.

Playing

The bidder begins play with one card, the suit of which becomes trumps for that hand.

Each person in turn plays one card, following suit if possible. If not, any other card may be played. The trick contains one card from each player and is won by the person who plays:

a) the highest trump card; or

b) the highest card of the leading suit.

Play continues until all five tricks have been made.

Scoring

The usual stakes are:

a) two counters for a bid of two

b) three counters for a bid of three

c) four counters for a bid of four

d) ten counters for a bid of napoleon

The other players each pay the bidder these stakes if he fulfils his contract. If he does not, he must pay each player the stake instead, except if he bid napoleon, in which case he pays each player half the stake.

Optional bids

Sometimes the game is played with the following bids:

a) 'Wellington' is a bid to win all five tricks for double stakes (20 counters). A wellington can only be bid following a bid of napoleon.

b) 'Blücher' will outbid a wellington for triple the stakes (30 counters).

c) 'Misère' or 'misery' is a bid to lose every trick and ranks between a bid of three and a bid of four. It carries a stake of three counters. Misery is played without trumps.

NAPOLEON VARIATIONS
PURCHASE NAP

The rules are as for napoleon, except that on payment of one counter per card, any player may exchange one or more of his cards for unseen cards from the top of the stock. The payments are set aside in a kitty to be won by the first player to fulfil a bid of napoleon.

SEVEN-CARD NAP

Play is the same as for napoleon, but each player is dealt seven cards and there are no bids of wellington or blücher.

The rank order of bids and their stakes is:

a) three bid: stake three

b) four bid: stake four

c) nap or misère bid: stake ten

d) six bid: stake 18

e) seven bid: stake 24

Only half the stake is paid if a player loses a bid of nap, misère, six or seven.

Oh hell

Similar to whist, oh hell is a game for three or more
players, each playing alone. Oh hell is also known as
blackout, and by some as oh well.

Cards

A standard 52-card deck is used, with ace ranking high.

Rank

high   low

Aim

Every player makes a bid for tricks, which he tries to
fulfil exactly.

Dealing

The player making the highest cut becomes the first
dealer. Subsequent deals pass clockwise; there are
several deals in each game. In the first deal players are
dealt one card each. In the next deal, players are dealt
two cards each; in the third, three cards; and so on.
When it is no longer possible to deal an extra card to
each player, the game ends. For example, when there
are four players there will be 13 deals; when there are
five players, 10 deals.

Trumps

The top card from the stock is turned up at the end of
each deal to designate trumps. When the last deal of
the game allows for no stock, there are no trumps in
that hand.

Bidding

The dealer begins by bidding the number of tricks he
expects to win or bidding 'nullo' if he does not expect
to make any.

In the first hand, the bid is one or nullo. The number of
possible bids increases as the number of dealt cards
increases.

Playing

The player to the dealer's left leads with any card. In
the first hand he has no choice but to play the single
card he has been dealt. The others must follow suit if
they can. If not, they may trump or discard.

The player winning the trick claims it face down and
leads to the next trick.

Scoring

Players who have fulfilled their bids exactly gain one
point per trick plus a bonus of 10 points.

For fulfilling a bid of nullo, the score may be five
points, or one point per trick in the hand plus five
points. Players should agree beforehand which scoring
system is to be used.

Players who make fewer or more than the number of
tricks bid do not score or lose penalty points.

Optional scoring

A bonus of 25 points can be won by a player who
fulfils a small slam bid by winning all but one of the

hand's tricks, providing there are more than five cards in the hand.

A bonus of 50 points can be won by a player who makes a grand slam (all the tricks).

Winning the game

The player with the highest total score after all deals are played is the winner.

Pinochle

Developed from bezique, pinochle is a game for two players. It is popular in North America and is also known as pinocle or penuchle.

Cards

Two standard 52-card decks are stripped of all cards below 9, leaving a deck of 48 cards. The cards rank ace, 10, K, Q, J and 9 from high to low.

Rank

high   low

Aim

Each person tries to make scoring melds and take tricks that contain high-scoring cards.

Dealing

The player making the highest cut becomes the first dealer. He shuffles the cards and asks the non-dealer to cut them before he deals 12 cards to the non-dealer and himself, in packets of three or four.

The trump suit for the hand is assigned by turning up the next card and placing it face up on the table.

If it is a 9, it is called the dix and the dealer gains 10 points immediately.

A stock is made by turning the remaining cards face down, partly obscuring the trump card.

The same trump remains throughout both stages of play.

Playing: stage one

The non-dealer plays a card to the first trick, followed by the dealer, who may play any card and does not have to follow suit.

The trick is won by the highest trump card or by the highest ranking card of the leading suit, if no trumps are played. If both cards in the trick are of the same suit and denomination, the one played first wins.

The winner of the trick places it face down in front of him. He may then claim a meld if he wishes.

Melding

During the first stage of play, the winner of each trick may claim a meld by placing the appropriate cards face up on the table and calling its name and score.

Melds

There are three classes of meld, with name and points values as shown.

Class A

Ace, 10, K, Q and J of trumps, 'sequence' or 'flush':	150 points
K and Q of trumps, 'royal marriage':	40 points
K and Q of a plain suit, 'marriage':	20 points

Class B

Q of spades and J of diamonds, 'pinochle':	40 points

Class C

Sets of four cards must contain one from each suit.

Four aces:	100 points
Four Ks:	80 points
Four Qs:	60 points
Four Js:	40 points

Melds when diamonds are trumps

Class A

150 points   40 points   20 points

Class B

40 points

Trump

Class C

100 points

80 points

60 points

40 points

Only one meld can be scored in each turn, although each melded card can be used to form a meld of a different class, or one of a higher score in the same class, at another turn. Each new meld formed from a previous meld must also contain a new card from the hand.

A player may use any of his melded cards to make tricks, but cards used for tricks cannot be used again to make melds.

Drawing from the stock

Whether he has made a meld or not, the player completes his turn by taking the top card from the stock. The other player then takes the next card from the stock.

The first stage of play continues until all the stock (including the trump card) has been taken. An optional rule of play is that the last face-down card should be revealed by whoever takes it.

The dix

The 9 of trumps is called the dix. If it was not turned up by the dealer and instead appears during the first stage of play, the person holding it may declare it, lay it down on the table and claim 10 points. It is usual to allow a meld to be made in the same turn. After winning a trick, the player may exchange the dix for the trump card under the stock.

Playing: stage two

Known as the playout, this stage requires each player to take back into his hand all the cards that remain in his melds on the table.

The player who won the last trick of the first stage leads a card for the first of 12 tricks in this stage.

The other player must follow suit if he can. If not, he may play a trump or discard. If the leading card is a trump, a higher trump must be played, if possible. Usually, the player following the lead tries to take the trick if he can.

No melds are made and the winner of one trick leads to the next.

Scoring tricks

At the end of each hand, tricks are scored according to the cards taken, as follows:

a) Ace: 11 points each
b) 10: 10 points each
c) K: 4 points each
d) Q: 3 points each
e) J: 2 points each

Points for tricks are rounded up to the nearest multiple of 10 if the units are 7, 8, 9 and rounded down if the units are below 7.

The player winning the final trick of the second stage of play gains an extra 10 points.

Scoring tricks

11 points   10 points   4 points   3 points   2 points

Winning the game

The player who first reaches a score of 1000 points wins the game. If both players pass the 1000-point total in the same hand, they play on until one reaches a score of 1250. If a draw happens again, play continues until 1500 points have been won, and so on, until there is one clear winner.

AUCTION PINOCHLE

In this variation, each player bids the number of points they expect to gain. Successful players win chips.

Players

Played at a table of four, the game calls for one player to act as dealer while the other three play against each other.

Dealing

Using a deck of 48 cards, as in standard pinochle, 15 cards are dealt in five packets of three to each player. After everyone has been dealt the first packet, a three-card widow is placed face down on the table.

Bidding

Beginning with the player to the dealer's left, each player bids the number of points he expects to gain. There is an agreed starting minimum bid (normally 300), and bidding rises by 10 points per bid.

Players must bid or pass. After passing, a player takes no further part in the bidding of that hand. Bidding continues until two players pass. The remaining player is known as the 'bidder' and his highest bid becomes the contract he is expected to fulfil. The other two players cooperate to try to prevent him from doing so.

Melding

Before play, the bidder takes the three widow cards into his hand, after displaying them to the others.

The bidder then declares the trump suit and lays his

melds on the table. In auction pinochle, only the bidder is allowed to make melds.

Melds are the same as for standard pinochle. The dix (9 of trumps) counts as an extra class A meld and scores 10 points. It can only be added to the bidder's score if he puts it on the table with his other melds.

Playing

After he has laid out his melds, the bidder discards, face down, three cards from his hand. Then he picks up his melded cards and leads the first trick with any card from his hand.

The bidder can change his decision about his melds, discards or trumps at any time before he starts the first trick.

If the bidder mistakenly tries to discard from a meld for which he has already scored, he must immediately correct his mistake, before leading the first trick. Otherwise he will forfeit the game.

Playing for tricks

The rules for standard pinochle apply. The players must follow suit if they can. If not, they must play a trump if they hold one. They must try to win the trick if a trump is led. If a trick has been trumped, the last player must also play a trump, but it need not be a higher trump. The winner of a trick leads the next one.

Scoring tricks

The bidder scores for any scoring cards among the three he discards; he also gains an extra 10 points if he is the one to win the last trick.

Players should decide whether to score as in standard pinochle or use one of the following scoring variations:

a) Aces and 10s: 10 points each; Ks and Qs: 5 points each; or

b) Aces, 10s and Ks: 10 points each.

Winning the game

A game consists of one hand only. The bidder wins chips, as follows, from each player if he fulfils or exceeds his contract:

Bid	Number of chips
300–340	3
350–390	5
400–440	10
450–490	15
500–540	20
550–590	25
600 or more	30

If spades are trumps, these scores are doubled.

The kitty

Auction pinochle usually has a kitty with the following rules:

a) players put in three chips each before play starts;

b) all players pay three chips each into the kitty, if all three pass during bidding; and

c) when the bidder makes a contract of 350 or more, he pays to the kitty if he fails, or takes from the kitty if he succeeds, in addition to collecting from or paying the other players. The amount is the same as the payments between players as listed (see Winning the game).

Piquet

This game offers two players the opportunity to use great skill. Known by various names since the 1450s, the game was given its French name and terminology by Charles I of England to honour Henrietta Maria, his French wife.

Modern piquet has some optional rules, sometimes called American style or English style. The options are described here when they occur. Most players generally choose one style and keep to it.

Cards

The piquet deck of 32 cards is used, which ranks normally with ace high. It is made by stripping the cards below 7 from a standard 52-card deck. Regular piquet players have two decks, one in use and the other ready shuffled for the next deal.

Rank

high   low

Aim

A player tries to score more points than his opponent by taking tricks and by collecting scoring combinations of cards.

Card values

| 11 points | 10 points each | 9 points | 8 points | 7 points |

Dealing

The player cutting the higher card becomes first dealer and chooses his seat. The dealer shuffles the cards which are then cut by the non-dealer.

Beginning with the non-dealer, each player is dealt 12 cards in packets of two. A stock is formed from the remaining eight cards by turning the cards face down and dividing them so that the upper five lie at an angle to the lower three.

The stock

The partie

A game is known as a partie and normally consists of six deals. Each deal has four parts:

a) making discards;

b) deciding which scoring combinations to declare;

c) announcing declarations; and

d) playing for tricks.

Scoring takes place as the partie unfolds, so paper and pencil are essential for keeping the scores and cumulative totals.

Scoring before the discard

After the deal, and before a player discards, he may claim 10 points if he has been dealt carte blanche (a hand with no court cards). English rules state a carte blanche score must be claimed before both players discard.

Making discards

The dealer discards first. American rules state he need not discard, but English rules say he must discard at least one card. Either way, a player may only discard up to five cards.

If the dealer decides to discard, he places the cards he wants to discard face down near him.

Drawing from the top of the stock, in order, he takes the same number of cards into his hand.

If the dealer chooses not to discard, or discards fewer than five cards, he has the right to look at all five top cards of the stock, replacing them in the same order. He does not show the cards to his opponent.

The non-dealer must then discard one card and may discard more, up to the number remaining in the whole stock. He places them face down beside him and takes replacements into his hand from the top of the stock in order.

He can then inspect the cards (if any) that remain in the stock, but if he does, the dealer may also inspect them. (Some players only allow the dealer to inspect them later, after he has played his first trick.)

During play, both players may inspect their own discards at any time.

Combinations to declare

Players can make three kinds of combinations, using the cards in their hands. Any card may be included in more than one combination. The aim is to make high-scoring combinations which rank higher than the opponent's combinations.

A player may choose to 'sink' one or more of his combinations by not declaring it. No score can be claimed for any combination that has been sunk.

There are three types of combination, called 'point', 'sequence' and 'meld'.

A point is a collection of cards all of the same suit. The player with the biggest collection scores one point for each card in that suit.

If both players have a collection of the same number, the cards in each collection are counted at face value and the highest score wins the point value. If there is still a draw, neither player scores. A player can only score for one point, even if he holds two collections greater than his opponent's.

Ranking when point scores are the same

point score is 4   point score is 4
face value is 36   face value is 35
this point ranks higher   this point ranks lower

A sequence is a run of three or more cards in one suit
in rank order. The player with the longest sequence
scores for all the sequences he holds, as follows:

a) three cards, a tierce: 3 points
b) four cards, a quart: 4 points
c) five cards, a quint: 15 points
d) six cards, a sextet or sixième: 16 points
e) seven cards, a septet or septième: 17 points
f) eight cards , an octet or huitième: 18 points

The loser makes no score for any of his sequences.
If there is a draw, the sequence with the highest
ranking top card wins. If there is still a draw, neither
player scores.

Sample sequences in rank order

lowest rank: 3 points

highest rank: 15 points

A meld is three or four cards of the same kind in different suits. Only aces, Ks, Qs, Js and 10s may be used in melds. Some players only allow 10s in melds of four cards.

The player making the longest meld scores for all the melds he holds as follows:

a) three cards, a trio: 3 points

b) four cards, a quatorze or 'fourteen': 14 points

If both players have melds of the same length, the one with the highest ranking cards wins.

Sample melds

3 points   14 points

Announcing declarations

The announcements are made briefly and formally to avoid revealing too much information. Declarations are made in the order of points, sequences and then melds. (Some players prefer the French names for sequences and melds.) The non-dealer begins each dialogue.

Dialogue declaring a point

Non-dealer: 'A point of..., ' saying how many cards are in his longest suit.

Dealer replies with either:

a) 'good' if he concedes the point;

b) 'not good...,' stating how many cards in his point if it is longer; or

c) 'how many?' if his suit is the same length.

Non-dealer continues with either:

a) 'a point of... I score...,' restating his point and its score;

b) 'good' conceding the point; or

c) if the dealer had asked 'how many?' he states the face value of his point, to which the dealer replies:

a) 'good' conceding the point;

b) 'not good...,' stating the face value of his point if greater and claiming the point score; or

c) 'equal' if the face value is the same. In this case, neither player scores.

The player who wins the point always ends by saying: 'A point of.... I score...,' giving the point value and its score.

Declaring a sequence

Non-dealer: 'A sequence of...,' stating the number of cards in his longest one.

The dealer replies with either 'Good,' 'Not good' or 'How high?' and the dialogue continues as for points. The reply to 'How high?' is to name the top card of the sequence.

Declaring a meld

The non-dealer begins by declaring 'A three (or a fourteen) of...,' stating the denomination of his meld. The reply can only be 'Good' or 'Not good' as players cannot have equal melds.

A sample declaration

The declaration of points, sequences and melds follow each other.

Non-dealer: 'A point of four.'

Dealer: 'Good.'

Non-dealer: 'A point of four. I score four. A quint

(sequence of five).'

Dealer: 'How high?'

Non-dealer: 'Jack.'

Dealer: 'Not good. Queen. Also a tierce (a sequence of three). I score eight.'

Non-dealer: 'A trio of queens (three queens).'

Dealer: 'Not good. A quatorze (fourteen in kings). I score fourteen. I start with 22.'

Non-dealer: 'I start with five.' He scored four for his point plus one for leading the first trick (see Scoring tricks).

A sample of English-style declaration

The dealer only declares his combinations after the non-dealer has led the first trick.

Non-dealer: 'A point of four.'

Dealer: 'Good.'

Non-dealer: 'A point of four. I score four. A sequence of five.'

Dealer: 'How high?'

Non-dealer: 'Jack.'

Dealer: 'Not good.'

Non-dealer: 'A trio of queens.'

Dealer: 'Not good.'

The non-dealer then plays the leading card to the first trick, saying: 'I start with five.'

The dealer then makes his declarations: 'A quart to queen, also a tierce. Eight. A quatorze of kings. Fourteen. I start with 22.'

Showing combinations

It is sometimes ruled that all the winning combinations must be shown before they are scored.

However, it is standard practice for a player to request

his opponent to show his combination, which is immediately replaced in the hand. If an opponent does not request a show, none is given.

Playing

The first trick is led by the non-dealer. Players must follow suit if possible. If not, any card may be discarded. The player winning the trick leads to the next one.

Scoring tricks

a) For leading to a trick: 1 point
b) For taking a trick led by the opponent: 1 point
c) For taking the last trick: 1 point
d) For taking seven or more tricks: 10 points

Every time a player scores, he records it and announces his running total.

There are some optional variations to scoring for tricks:

1) a player only scores for leading to a trick if the leading card is 10 or higher;
2) a player only scores for winning a trick if the winning card is 10 or higher.

Scoring additional points

a) Carte blanche (a hand with no
court cards at the deal):   10 points
b) Pique (a score of 30 points by
the non-dealer before the dealer
scores anything):   30 bonus points
c) Repique (a score of 30 points by
either player before the lead to the
first trick):   60 bonus points
d) Capot (taking all 12 tricks during
play):   40 bonus points

The player cannot also claim the 10 points for taking

seven or more tricks (see Scoring tricks).

Scoring the partie (game)

1) The scores for each deal are added together to give players their individual total. If a partie consists of six games, six totals will be added. Some people prefer a partie of four games. In this case the scores for the first and the last deals are doubled before the four totals are added.

2) If both players have reached or exceeded the rubicon (100 points), the winner is the player with the higher total.

The winner's score then becomes the difference between his and his opponent's totals, plus a bonus of 100 points for winning the partie.

3) If one or both players have totals of fewer than 100 points, the player with the lower total is 'rubiconed'. The other player is the winner and his score then becomes the sum of his and his opponent's totals, plus a bonus of 100 points for winning the partie.

Sample scores

	Totals	Final score	
Dealer	120	120-108+100 = 112	Winner
Non-dealer	108	Nil	
Dealer	95	Nil	
Non-dealer	125	125+95+100 = 325	Winner
Dealer	82	Nil	
Non-dealer	85	85+82+100 = 267	Winner

PIQUET VARIATIONS
PIQUET AU CENT

This variation of piquet has a different final method of scoring. There is no fixed number of deals; instead, play continues until one player has reached 100 points. When the hand in which 100 points are reached is complete, the game ends.

The winner is the player with the higher total. His final score is the difference between his own and his opponent's totals. If his opponent's total is less than 50, the winner doubles his final score.

AUCTION PIQUET

This version concentrates on the playing of the hands. Players bid for tricks.

Bidding

Before the discard, the non-dealer makes a bid or passes. The dealer reshuffles and makes another deal if both players pass. When a bid has been made, bidding continues until one person passes.

The smallest bid is seven. A bid may be a plus or a minus, to win or lose the stated number of tricks. Plus and minus bids rank equally, and the highest number wins the contract, which the bidder aims to fulfil.

Doubling and redoubling

A player may say 'double' after any of his opponent's bids, indicating that he thinks he can prevent the bidder from fulfilling the bid, if it became the contract. When a bid has been 'doubled', the bidder may call 'redouble' if he is confident he can fulfil his bid. Both a doubled and a redoubled bid can be outbid, but if not the final score will be affected.

Differences in playing

The rules for the rest of the game are the same as for standard piquet, except as follows:

a) players need not discard;

b) declarations can be made in any order;

c) a player may not sink (withhold a declaration) on a minus contract;

d) pique is scored after 21 points in a minus contract and 29 points in a plus contract;

e) repique is scored after 21 points in a minus contract and 30 points in a plus contract.

Differences in scoring

A player gains a point for every trick he takes, even if he did not lead to it.

Leading to a trick and taking the last trick do not give extra scores.

Scoring the contract

The bidding player scores 10 points for every trick he wins (on plus contracts) or loses (on minus contracts) that are in excess of his contract.

A player's opponent scores 10 points for every trick the bidder fails to make (on a plus) or lose (on a minus) to fulfil his contract.

Scoring doubling and redoubling

If the bidder fails to fulfil a doubled contract, he doubles the score for tricks made above his bid on a plus contract and for extra tricks lost on a minus contract. These are both called overtricks.

If the bidder fails to fulfil a doubled contract, his opponent gains double the score on the tricks the bidder failed to make (on a plus contract) or failed to lose (on a minus contract). These are called undertricks.

If a contract has been redoubled, then the doubled scores for overtricks and undertricks, as described for a doubled contract, are doubled.

Scoring the partie

The bonus for the partie is 150 points; rubicon is 150 points.

Pope Joan

A game for three or more players in which cards are
played in order to gain counters. Once very popular in
Scotland, Pope Joan is a combination of two earlier
games called commit and matrimony.

Cards

The 8 of diamonds is removed from a standard deck,
leaving 51 cards. Aces rank low and the 9 of diamonds
is known as Pope Joan.

Rank

Pope Joan

high   low

Preparing

Each player should begin with an equal number of
counters with which to bet. A betting layout or board
with eight sections will be needed. Some traditional
boards for Pope Joan are revolving circular trays
divided into eight segments.

For a modern board, a square layout with eight sections

can be drawn on paper or card as shown. The sections should be labelled king, queen, jack, ace, matrimony, game, intrigue and Pope Joan. They should be large enough to hold about 20 counters each.

Square layout

Aim

Certain cards are played in order to win counters. The player first using up all his cards also wins counters.

Betting

A dealer is chosen by agreement. All players then place counters on the betting layout in one of two ways, again by agreement:

a) everyone places the same number of counters on each section; or

b) everyone places four players on Pope Joan, two on intrigue, two on matrimony and one on each of the other five sections.

Betting

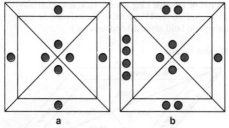

a   b

Dealing

The cards are dealt clockwise, one at a time and face down, beginning with the player to the dealer's left. An extra hand is dealt immediately before the dealer's own hand. All but one card is dealt out. This last card is placed exposed on top of the widow.

The exposed card

The standard rule is that if this exposed card is Pope Joan (9 of diamonds), all the counters in the game and pope sections of the board go to the dealer.

Alternatively, some players agree the dealer should win all counters on the layout. Either way, that round ends and the deal passes to the player on the dealer's left.

If the exposed card is any card other than Pope Joan, its suit is the trump suit for that round.

If the exposed card is an ace or a court card, all counters on the corresponding section of the board go to the dealer, and the round continues.

Playing

The extra hand may not be inspected. The player to the dealer's left plays any card from his hand face up in the centre of the table, announcing its name – e.g. '3 of clubs'.

The player holding the 4 of clubs plays and announces it. Then the players with the 5, the 6 and so on play those cards. A player holding two or more cards in sequence plays them all, announcing each one. The sequence continues until:

a) the K has been reached and the sequence is complete;
b) the next card would need to be the 8 of diamonds; or
c) the next card has already been played or is hidden in the extra hand.

The sequence is then turned face down and may not be inspected. The person playing the last card begins another sequence with any card from his hand.

Claiming counters

Certain cards win counters when played in correct sequence.

The ace, J, Q or K of trumps win all the counters on the section of the same name. The J and Q of trumps, played in sequence, win the counters on the intrigue, jack and queen sections.

The Q and K of trumps, played together, win the counters on matrimony, queen and king.

If Pope Joan is played, the player claims the counters on that section, whether it is the trump suit or not.

None of these cards can score if they remain in the hand.

Ending a round

When someone has played all his cards, the round ends and he takes the counters from the game section. All other players pay him one counter for each card they are still holding. The only exemption is a player left holding Pope Joan, who does not pay for any cards in his hand. At the end of each round, unclaimed counters remain in place. At the beginning of each round, counters are added before the deal.

Winning the game

The game usually continues to an agreed time limit. Then a final deal is made, excluding the extra hand and including the last card, to determine who shall claim any remaining counters.

The players receiving the ace, J, Q and K of diamonds, and the Pope Joan, claim the counters on those sections. Any counters in matrimony are shared between the players holding the K and Q of diamonds; counters in intrigue go equally to the holders of the J and Q.

Preference

A simple card game for three players who usually play for small stakes.

Cards

A 32-card deck is make by stripping all cards below the 7s from a standard deck. Ace ranks high.

The suits are also ranked: hearts (high), diamonds, clubs, spades (low). Hearts are known as the preference suit.

Rank

high   low

preference suit

Aim

Individuals attempt to make the highest bid and then fulfil it.

Preparing

An agreed number of counters are put into the pool by each player.

Players must also agree about:

a) the number of counters paid from the pool to the successful bidder, for each suit;

b) the amount paid into the pool by a bidder who fails to fulfil his contract.

Dealing

Players agree who shall be first dealer. After shuffling the cards, he deals a packet of three cards, face down, to each player, beginning with the player to his left. He then deals a widow of two cards, face down, in the centre of the table.

Finally he deals each player a packet of four cards and another packet of three. Each player should have a hand of 10 cards.

In subsequent rounds, the deal passes clockwise round the table and is carried out in the same way.

Bidding

Starting with the player to the dealer's left, each player either bids a suit or passes. The number of tricks expected to be won is not part of the bid; instead, players bid the suit they believe they can use as trumps to make at least six tricks. They can bid only once, and they must bid a higher-ranking suit than the previous player.

If all players pass on the first round, they go to a second round of bidding. Players then either pass or place second counters in the pool. The person placing the highest number of counters wins the bid and names the trump suit. The winning bidder can then discard two cards and pick up the widow if he chooses. If any

bid is made in the first round, the widow is left
untouched.

Playing

The player on the left of the bidder plays one card to
lead the first trick. Everyone must follow suit. If a
player cannot do this, he may use a trump or discard.
The highest trump or the highest card of the leading
suit wins the trick. The winner of one trick leads to the
next. When all 10 tricks have been taken, the
settlement takes place.

Settling

If the bidder fulfils his bid to take at least six tricks, he
is paid the agreed number of counters from the pool,
according to the suit.

If he fails to fulfil his bid, he pays into the pool the
agreed number of counters.

Rummy

Internationally one of the most popular card games, rummy evolved from rum poker, which was played in 19th-century saloons in the USA.

Players

Any number from two to six, each person playing for himself.

Cards

The standard deck of 52 cards is used and ace ranks low. J, Q and K of each suit are worth 10 points each; all other cards are face value, with ace worth one point. Melds are made by:

a) grouping three or four cards of the same rank; or

b) making a sequence of three or more cards of the same suit.

Melds

a group

b sequence

Aim

Individuals try to be first to go out by melding all their cards.

Preparing

The first dealer is chosen by low cut. He then shuffles the cards and invites the player on his right to cut the

pack. A winning score is agreed (see Scoring) and
scores are kept on paper.

Dealing

Cards are dealt singly in clockwise rotation, the number
depending on how many players there are:

a) two players are each dealt 10 cards;

b) three to four players are each dealt 7 cards;

c) five to six players are each dealt 6 cards. A stock is
made by turning the pile of undealt cards face down. A
discard pile is begun by turning up the top card from
the stock and placing this up-card on the table, next to
the stock.

Playing

The player to the left of the dealer begins by choosing
to take either the upcard or the top card from the stock.
He may then lay face up on the table any meld he
holds. Finally, a card must be discarded. This can be
any card except the one taken from the discard pile.
Play proceeds clockwise. After laying down melds,
players may additionally lay-off extra cards on melds
already formed by other players.

The round ends when a player goes out - i.e. uses up all
his cards, with or without a final discard. A player goes
rummy when he goes out all in one hand without any
previous melding or laying off of cards.

If no player has gone out before the stock is used up, a
new stock is made by turning the discard pile face
down, without shuffling.

After a player has gone out, there is a new deal for the
next round. The deal passes clockwise from the first
dealer.

Scoring

When a player goes out, his score is the combined numerical value of all his opponents' cards in hand. When a player goes rummy, the score is doubled.

Winning the game

The first player to reach the agreed score wins the match.

GIN RUMMY

A simple, fast, two-handed variation of rummy. The rules are the same as for rummy except as described here.

Cards

Two standard decks of cards are used, one being dealt while the other is being shuffled by another player in readiness for the next round. The cards rank normally with ace low.

Rank

high   low

Players

Standard gin rummy is for two players. It can be played by any number of people, by dividing the players into two sides. Pairs can then play against each other simultaneously.

Aim

Each player tries to meld all his cards, but a player can still win under certain circumstances even when he does not meld all his cards.

Preparing

Pencil and paper should be to hand for scoring.

Players agree to one of the following:

a) the number of rounds to be played;

b) a maximum score; or

c) a time limit on the match.

Dealing

The person cutting the higher card can choose which deck to use, where to sit and if he wants to deal.

Beginning with his opponent, he deals 10 cards each, singly and face down. The 21st card is turned up and this upcard starts the discard pile. The other cards are placed face down to form the stock pile.

Playing

The non-dealer can take the upcard if he wants it. If not, the dealer may take it. If he does not, the non-dealer must take a card from the stock.

The players take a card in turn, and must discard one, building melds in their hands. No melds are laid on the table until one player 'goes knocking' or 'goes gin' when it is his turn, or until only two cards are left in the stock.

Ending the round

a) Going gin happens when a player melds all 10 cards.

b) Knocking is an option when the value of unmelded cards totals 10 or less. To knock, a player draws a card at his turn, knocks on the table and throws away one card. Melds and unmelded cards are laid down. The other player then puts down his cards and can lay off any of his unmelded cards on the opponent's melds.

c) A tie is declared and a new hand dealt by the same dealer when two cards remain in the stock and the last player cannot go gin or knock. No points are scored. When the round is over, a line is drawn under or around the score of the player winning that hand. This is called a box.

Scoring points

Scores for each hand and a running total are kept for each player. Points can be gained in four ways:

1) a gin gains 25 points plus the value of the loser's unmelded cards;

2) a player who knocks gets the difference in value between the unmelded cards of the two players unless his opponent has an unmelded card count equal to or greater than his. Then the opponent gets the points plus a bonus of 25 points;

3) every box (winning hand) nets 25 points;

4) a bonus of 100 points is gained by the player to first reach 100 points in a game.

Sample of scoring sheet for one game

Hand	Player A score total	Player B score total
1st	11 – 11	0 – 0
2nd	0 – 11	5 – 5
3rd	19 – 30	0 – 5
4th	0 – 30	27 – 32
5th	25 – 55	0 – 32
6th	21 – 76	0 – 32
7th	45 – 121	0 – 32
Total	121	32
Game bonus	100	
Boxes	125	50
Total score	346	84

Scotch whist

Not at all like whist, this game is often called catch the ten.

Players

Any number from two to six people each play for himself. If there are four players, they may prefer to play in partnerships.

Cards

A deck of 36 cards is made by stripping all the 2s, 3s, 4s and 5s from a standard 52-card deck. Ace ranks high in both plain and trump suits, but the J ranks highest when a suit is trumps. A trick consists of one card from each person played in turn.

Rank when spades are trumps

high   low

Rank when spades is a plain suit

high   low

Aim

Each player tries to win as many tricks as he can, especially those containing high-scoring trump cards.

Dealing

The player making the highest cut becomes the first dealer and decides the seating positions. He shuffles the cards, inviting the player on his right to cut the cards.

Beginning with the player on his left and proceeding clockwise, he deals cards singly, face down. If there are two or three players, each is dealt 10 cards.

If there are four or more players, the whole deck is dealt. When there are four players they receive nine cards each, and the last card dealt to the dealer is turned up to determine the trump suit for that hand.

Five players will be dealt seven cards each, and the 36th card will be turned up to determine trumps before being dealt to the next player in turn, who will then have a hand of eight cards. Six players will receive six cards each and the dealer's last card will determine trumps.

Playing

The player to the left of the dealer begins by playing any card from his hand. Players follow suit in turn. If they cannot follow suit, they may trump or discard. The trick is won by:

a) the highest trump card; or

b) the highest card of the leading suit.

The player winning a trick leads to the next one. Play continues in this way until all cards have been played. If there are five players, the final trick will consist of six cards.

Scoring

At the end of a hand, certain trump cards earn points.
Players holding these cards can score for them as
follows, but only if they are played:

J of trumps: 11 points
10 of trumps: 10 points
Ace of trumps: 4 points
K of trumps: 3 points
Q of trumps: 2 points

Players also score one card point for every card taken
in tricks in excess of the number they were dealt. For
example:

dealt 10, taken 15 in tricks: 5 points
dealt 6, taken 18 in tricks: 12 points

If a player fails to follow the rules of play, he is not
allowed to score in that deal and has 10 points
deducted from his score.

Winning the game

The first person who reaches a score of 41 points wins
the game. If two players reach a total of 41 in the same
hand, the winner is decided by scoring the points in this
order: 10 of trumps, card points, ace, K, Q and J of
trumps.

Seven up

A 17th-century English game for two or three players,
seven up is also known as high-low-jack, all fours and
old sledge.

Cards

A standard deck of 52 cards is used, the ace ranking
high.

Rank

high   low

Aim

Players try to win the game by scoring seven points.

Dealing

The first dealer is the player making the highest cut,
and he deals six cards, face down, to each player in two
packets of three.

The next card is turned face up to indicate the trump
suit. If it is any of the Js, the dealer wins one point.
Subsequent deals pass clockwise around the table.

The trump suit

The player to the dealer's left calls 'stand' if he is
satisfied with the trump suit. Play then begins.

If not, he says 'I beg' and the dealer has to choose to
keep or to change trumps.

If he keeps the trumps, he replies 'take one'. The

player who begged then scores one point and play begins.

If the dealer chooses to change trumps, he puts the face-up card to one side and deals a packet of three more cards to each player, turning the next card up to indicate the new trump suit.

If it is the same suit as the first trump, then the dealer repeats the procedure of dealing another three cards to each player and turning up the next card, until a new suit is indicated as trumps. If the deck runs out before a new trump is turned up, the cards are thrown in, shuffled and redealt. If the extra deal produces a new trump suit, play begins. If this card is a J, the dealer wins a point, providing it is not of the same suit as the first trump.

Discarding

After the trump has been set, players must discard all but six cards from their hands.

Playing

Play is the same as whist. The player to the left of the dealer plays one card to lead to the first trick. Players must each follow suit if possible. If not, they may use a trump or discard.

The winner of one trick leads to the next one. Play continues until all six tricks are made. Each player claims his own tricks, keeping them near him, face down.

Scoring

Tricks are turned face up for scoring at the end of each round. One point can be won for each of the following:
a) a 'high' (to the player dealt the highest trump);
b) a 'low' (to the player dealt the lowest trump);

c) a 'jack' (to the player who takes a trick containing the J of trumps); and

d) 'game' (to the player with the highest value of cards won in tricks).

Cards each carry a points value as follows:

Ace:	4 points
K:	3 points
Q:	2 points
J:	1 points
10:	10 points

Winning the game

The game is won by the first player to make seven points. If there is a draw of seven points each in the same hand, the points are counted in order, as follows, to decide who is the winner: high, low, jack, game.

SEVEN UP VARIATIONS

FOUR-HANDED SEVEN UP

Four people play in pairs, partners sitting opposite each other. Play proceeds as in the standard game except that the two players to the right may only look at their cards after the trump suit has been decided.

CALIFORNIA JACK

Sometimes called draw seven or California loo, this game is for two players. It has the following differences from the standard game.

Trumps

Trumps are always the first card turned up, but there is a new trump suit for each trick. First the winner, and then the loser, of each trick takes a card from the top of the stock. The next card is then turned up to determine trumps for the next trick.

When all the stock is used, players continue making tricks, and using the last trump as trumps, until their cards are played. The winner of one trick leads to the next.

Scoring

Each of the following, taken in tricks, scores one point: highest trump;
lowest trump; and
J of trumps.

The winner is the first player to score 10 points.

Skat

Skat is a game of great skill, and was developed in
19th-century Germany. The less complex rauber skat,
described here, is now popular throughout the western
world.

Players

Three of up to five people play in each deal. The active
players are called forehand, middlehand and endhand,
while the fourth player and the dealer sit out. If there
are only three people forehand deals.

Five people

a forehand
b middlehand
c endhand
d fourth player
e dealer

Three people

Cards

The standard deck is reduced to 32 by removing all
cards below 7. Ace ranks high.

Ranking of all suits without trumps

high   low

When a suit is declared trumps, the 10 ranks above the
K in all suits and all Js become the top-ranking trumps,
their suits ranking clubs (high), spades, hearts,
diamonds (low).

Ranking with spades as trumps

Trumps   high   low

Ranking of all other suits with spades as trumps

high   low

Aim

Players bid against each other to name the game. The
winning bidder plays to win, while his opponents try to
stop him.

Preparing

Pencil and paper will be needed for scoring.

The player with the highest cut becomes the dealer.

The others play forehand, middlehand and endhand, in
order from the dealer's left. Subsequent deals and
playing positions pass clockwise to the next player.

Dealing

The dealer shuffles and invites the player on his left to
cut the pack. Beginning from the forehand player, the
active players are each dealt a packet of three cards,
face down.

Two cards are then placed face down in the centre of the
table to form the skat.

Players are finally dealt a packet of four cards each
followed by a packet of three, making a total hand of
10 cards each.

Bidding

The bid is a player's estimate of the game points he
expects to score playing his chosen game. The
minimum bid is 18; a realistic maximum is 100.

'Pass' means a player is opting out of the bidding and
may not bid again during that deal.

'Hold' means a player is accepting the last bid.

Middlehand begins the bidding against forehand.

1) Middlehand passes or makes a game score bid.

2) Forehand must either pass or hold.

3) Middlehand must then either pass or raise his bid.

4) Forehand again either passes or holds.

The two continue until one gives way by passing.
The winner from this pair then meets endhand, who
starts the bidding again, which proceeds as before.
Finally, a winning bidder emerges. If it is forehand, he
may make a final bid of his own or close the bidding
by passing, in which case there is a new deal.

The skat

The winning bidder may pick up the skat. If he does, he
must discard two cards from his hand, although both
will count in his final score. Alternatively, the winning
bidder may decide to go 'handplay' by leaving the skat
out of play.

Choosing the game

There are five games: suits, grand, simple null, open
null and reject. A bidder who has picked up the skat
may only choose suits or grand.

Suits

The bidder names the trump suit, which also makes the
four Js trump cards. He then aims to make 61 trick
points with high-scoring cards.

Grand
The only trumps are the four Js and the aim is to make
61 trick points with high-scoring cards.

Simple null
A game without trumps in which the bidder tries to lose
every trick.

Open null
A game without trumps in which the bidder aims to lose
every trick but must play with all his cards face up on
the table.

Reject
Only forehand may choose this game if he has won the
bid because the other two passed without bidding.
The only trumps are the four Js, and every player tries
to make a lower trick score than the others.

Extra choices
1) If the bidder has chosen handplay, he can increase his
game score by opting to play open suits or open grand. He
must lay his cards face up as he declares his game choice.
2) If the bidder has chosen suits or grand he can raise his
bid before the opening lead by calling:
a) 'schneider', a bid to win 91 points from the tricks; or
b) 'schwarz', a bid to win every trick.

Playing
Forehand plays one card face up on the table, known as
the opening lead. Middlehand, then endhand, must follow
suit, each laying one card face up on the table. If they
cannot follow suit, they may play a trump suit if a trump
suit has been declared, or they may discard. The highest
ranking card wins the trick. Whoever wins the trick of
three cards leads the next trick. Play proceeds until 10
tricks have been made.

Scoring trick cards

The point values of cards taken in tricks are:

Aces: 11 points
10s: 10 points
Ks: 4 points
Qs: 3 points
Js: 2 points

These are the only scoring cards.

Scoring trick cards

11 points   10 points   4 points

3 points   2 points   0 points

Scoring the skat

When 10 tricks have been completed, the skat cards
may be taken as follows and their point values included
in the score:

a) after suits or grand, the bidder takes the skat, or his
two discards if he already took the skat before play;

b) after reject, the skat goes to the winner of the last
trick;

c) After null games, the skat is discarded.

Making the game

A player makes the game when he achieves the aim of
the game to make 61 trick points, 91 trick points, all
tricks or no tricks. Then he must calculate if he has
made the number of game points he bid. The reject
game has no bidder, so is scored differently.

Making a bid

A bid is said to be 'made' providing the number of
game points stated in a bid exceeds or is the same as the
bidder's game score. Game points for suits, grand, null
and open null are as follows:

a) simple null has a fixed value of 23 points, open null
of 24;

b) the values of suit or grand games are determined by
multiplying a base game value by a multiplier (see Base
game values and Multipliers). The player makes his bid
if his total game value exceeds or equals his bid.

Base game values

diamonds:	9 points
hearts:	10 points
spades:	11 points
clubs:	12 points
grand:	20 points

Multipliers

a) making game:	1
b) matadors (see next paragraph):	at least 1
c) handplay:	1
d) schneider made but not declared:	1
e) schneider declared and made:	3
f) schneider declared and schwarz made:	4
g) schwarz made but not declared:	2
h) schwarz declared and made:	5

A player adds together all his multipliers; his total will be from 2 to 14. This total is multiplied by his base game value.

Matadors

Matadors are the top trump cards held in sequence by the bidder, together with the J of clubs. Trump cards from the skat are included, even if the skat was not used in play. The bidder's hand is said to be 'with matadors' if he holds the J of clubs, and 'without matadors' if he does not. The multiplier is the number of matadors the bidder's hand is with or without, as shown in the sample hands.

a) When spades are trumps, the hand is with three matadors. The missing J of diamonds breaks the sequence. Three is the multiplier.

b) When hearts are trumps, the hand is without two matadors. The two top trumps are missing. Two is the multiplier.

Matadors in sample hands

trumps   cards in hand

trumps   cards in hand

Scoring

The bidder scores as follows in all games but reject. Total game points (which may be higher than his bid) are won if he has made his bid.

If he fails to make his bid, he loses the following points:
a) for suits or grand: points equivalent to his bid if he chose handplay; double those points if he took the skat.
b) for null, the absolute game value.

Scoring reject

There is no bid or bidder in reject. It is usual for the player who makes the lowest number of tricks to score 10, except as follows:

a) taking no tricks nets 20;

b) a tie for the fewest trick points is resolved by giving the 10 points to the player who did not take the last trick;

c) taking all the tricks incurs a penalty of 30 points and nobody else scores; and

d) when all players tie with 40 trick points, only forehand scores the 10, for naming the game.

Winning the game

Scores are totalled and the person with the highest score wins. If it is preferred to play for counters or coins, it is usual to calculate the average score. Players with scores below average pay out, and those with scores above average collect.

Spoil five

A favourite game in the Republic of Ireland, spoil five
is much like loo, but the cards are ranked in a very
unusual way. Counters are used for scoring.

Players

The ideal number of players (each playing for himself)
is five or six, although any number from two upwards
can play.

Cards

A standard deck of 52 cards is used and the ranking
changes according to suit and status. Ranking is as
follows from high to low.

Clubs and spades

Plain: K, Q, J, ace, 2, 3, 4, 5, 6, 7, 8, 9, 10.

Trumps: 5, J, ace hearts, ace, K, Q, 2, 3, 4, 6, 7, 8, 9, 10.

Diamonds

Plain: K, Q, J, 10, 9, 8, 7, 6, 5, 4, 3, 2, ace.

Trumps: 5, J, ace hearts, ace, K, Q, 10, 9, 8, 7, 6, 4, 3, 2.

Hearts

Plain: K, Q, J, 10, 9, 8, 7, 6, 5, 4, 3, 2.

Trumps: 5, J, ace, K, Q, 10, 9, 8, 7, 6, 4, 3, 2.

When hearts is a plain suit, there is no ace because the
ace of hearts always takes third rank in all trump suits.

Rank in trumps

spades (or clubs)

diamonds

hearts

Rank in plain suits

spades (or clubs)

diamonds

hearts

Aim

Individuals try to win three tricks while keeping their opponents from doing so.

The pool

Players agree on how many counters are to be put in the pool whenever a contribution is made. Before the first deal, everyone puts in the same number of counters.

Dealing

Using standard ranking with ace high and 2 low, the players cut for deal. The lowest card determines the dealer. Beginning with the player to the dealer's left and moving clockwise, five cards are dealt face down to each player in packets of two then three or three then two. Trumps is determined by the next card, which is turned face up.

Exchanging and robbing

When the upcard is an ace, the dealer may 'rob' it by exchanging it for any card in his hand before the next trick is led.

If the ace of trumps is dealt to a player, he may trade the upcard for any card in his hand.

A player holding the ace of trumps must declare it at his first turn if he has not made an exchange. If he fails to do so, the ace automatically ranks lowest of the trumps for that hand, even if it is the ace of hearts.

Playing

The player on the dealer's left begins by playing the leading card. Each person plays one card to each trick. The trick is won by the highest ranking card of the leading suit or of the trump suit if a trump is used. The winner leads to the next trick.

If the leading card is a plain suit, all players may choose to follow suit or trump but may only discard if they cannot do either.

If the lead is a trump card, players must follow suit if they can, but may 'renege' by holding back any of the top three trumps, providing the lead card was a lower trump.

Jinxing

When a player wins three tricks, he may take the pool and end the hand, or he may 'jinx', meaning play will continue and he will try to win the remaining two tricks.

If he succeeds, he takes the pool and from each player the same number of counters as they each put into the pool.

If he fails to take both remaining tricks, he loses the pool and the round is considered a 'spoil'.

A spoil

A hand is called a spoil when nobody wins three tricks or the player who jinxes fails. The pool remains and the player to the left of the previous dealer becomes the new dealer; only he contributes to the pool. If there is no spoil, the pool is won and everyone puts counters in for the next hand.

Vint

A game related to whist for four players in pairs.

Cards

A standard deck of 52 cards is used. Ace ranks high.
The suits rank: no trumps, hearts, diamonds, clubs and
spades in descending order.

Rank of suits

no trumps

high   low

Aim

Partners try to make the highest bid and take tricks to
fulfil it.

Dealing

The dealer is chosen by high cut and the whole deck is
dealt, one card face down to each player in turn
clockwise. The deal rotates clockwise each round.

Bidding

The dealer begins by bidding or passing, followed by
each player.

Players bid the number of tricks above six they expect
to make, and the suit of those tricks.

The highest bid would be '7 no trumps' (for 13 tricks).

The lowest bid would be 'one, spades' (for 7 tricks).

A higher-ranking bid overcalls one of lower rank – i.e.

'8 diamonds' would be outbid by '8 hearts' or 9
diamonds'.

When a player's bid is overcalled he can make a higher
bid in the next round, even overcalling his partner.

The suit named in the highest ranking bid becomes
trumps, unless no trumps is the winning bid.

Playing

The player to the dealer's left leads play with one card
and each player follows with a card of the same suit in
turn clockwise. If a player cannot follow suit he may
use a trump or discard. The player winning the trick
leads to the next one.

Scoring

A score pad is used, with a central horizontal line, as in
bridge. Game points are entered below the line and
honour and bonus points above it.

Scorepad

We	They

Trick values and game points

Both partnerships score for the tricks they take. The
score per trick depends on the bid: each trick is worth
10 points on a bid of one, 20 points on a bid of two,
and so on to 70 points on a bid of seven.

The total score for tricks is called the game score and is
entered below the line. The game is won by the
partnership first to reach 500 points.

Bonus points

The bonus points are recorded above the line when a partnership wins the following:points

a) a game: 1000 points
b) a rubber (two out of three games): 2000 points
c) a little slam (12 tricks), not bid: 1000 points
d) a little slam, bid: 6000 points
e) a grand slam (13 tricks), not bid: 2000 points
f) a grand slam, bid: 12,000 points

Honour points

Points are scored for honour cards won in tricks. Honour cards are the ace, K, Q, J and 10 of trumps and all other aces. If an ace is in the trump suit it counts twice, as a trump and as an ace.

If there are no trumps, the only honour cards are the four aces.

Only the partnership with the most honours scores points as follows:

a) for honours in trumps: 10 times the trick value
b) for honours no trumps: 25 times the trick value

For example, if four trumps was the bid, honours score 10x40 = 400 points; if four no trumps was bid, honours score 25x40 = 1000 points.

To determine which partnership, on balance, has the most honours, the aces are compared with other honours as follows:

Side X: 2 honours + 1 ace; Side Y: 1 honour + 3 aces
X's two honours are deducted from Y's three aces.
Result: X has one ace, Y has one honour and one ace.
The aces cancel each other out, leaving the balance with side Y, who scores for one honour at 10 times the trick value.

When numbers are equal, they cancel each other out:

Side X: 3 honours + 1 ace

Side Y: 1 honour + 3 ace

In this case, neither side scores.

If both sides have two aces, the side with most tricks
scores its honour points if the bid was in trumps;
neither scores if the bid was no trumps.

Honours score above the line.

Coronet

A coronet is either three aces or a sequence of three
cards in a plain suit. These score 500 points above the
line. The fourth ace or a fourth card in the sequence
both score a further 500 points.

A sequence in the trump suit, or in any suit in a no
trump bid, scores as a double coronet.

Failure to make a bid

Every undertrick carries a penalty of 100 times the trick
value, which is entered as a minus score above the line,
although each trick taken still scores trick points below
the line.

If side X bids five no trumps (11 tricks) but makes only
eight tricks, it would score 15,000 penalty points
(3x50x100) and 400 trick points (8x50).

Whist

Whist became popular when Edmond Hoyle described it
in the first published rule book of card games in1746. It
was a refinement of the older game of triumph,
sometimes called whisk. Whist has since spawned many
challenging games such as solo whist and contract
bridge.

Players

Four people play in pairs. Partners sit opposite each
other.

Cards

The standard deck of 52 is used. Ace ranks high. A set of
four cards, one played in turn from each player, is a trick.

Aim

Partners cooperate to win tricks.

Preparing

The first dealer is chosen by high cut for which ace ranks
low. Any player can shuffle the cards before the dealer
makes the final shuffle and invites the player on his
right to cut the pack.

Dealing

The whole pack is dealt in clockwise direction. Cards
are dealt singly, face down, except the last one which is
turned up to assign trumps for that hand. The dealer
claims this card when he makes his first play.

There is a misdeal if any player receives fewer or more
than 13 cards or if any but the last card is revealed.
Players can agree to proceed after mistakes are corrected,
or a redeal can be claimed before the first trick is played.
The redeal passes to the next player clockwise.

Playing

The first player to the left of the dealer leads the play by laying a card face up in the middle of the table. Each person in turn plays one card of the leading suit face up. Anyone who cannot follow suit may use a trump or any other card.

The trick is won by the person playing:

a) the highest trump card; or

b) the highest ranking card of the leading suit.

Sample tricks

a leading suit clubs

ace clubs takes the trick

8 clubs takes the trick

b leading suit hearts, diamonds trumps

2 diamonds takes the trick

The winner claims the trick by turning it face down in front of him, and leads play for the next trick. The game continues until the hand of 13 tricks has been completed.

If all 13 tricks are won by one partnership, it is called a slam.

Subsequent deals for each new hand pass clockwise to the next player, who shuffles as before. A new trump suit is declared at each deal.

Conventions

a) A revoke is caused by not playing the leading suit when able to do so. It may be corrected without penalty before the trick is turned over. Penalty points can be demanded if the trick has been turned over. The whole hand is abandoned for a new deal if both partnerships revoke.

b) A card exposed when not being played must be left face up on the table. The opposition then call at their discretion for it to be played during the hand. It may not be used to make a revoke.

Common techniques include:

a) finessing by playing the third highest of a suit when also holding the highest;

b) leading with a trump when holding five or more;

c) leading the fourth best of the longest suit;

d) showing that ace is held by leading K; and

e) playing low as second player and high as third player.

Scoring game points

Game points can be won from tricks, honour cards and penalties. Partnerships keep a record of the number of tricks made in each hand. The first six tricks do not score. Tricks seven to thirteen score one game point each, for example:

Tricks in each hand: 6 7 2 10 8 4 etc.
Game points from hand: 0 1 0   4 2 0

From this stage onwards scoring systems differ. The two most common are described here.

The seven-point game is used in America. In addition to points from tricks, partners who revoke give the opposition two game points. The final score for each game is the difference between seven and the losers' total. The final hand, after seven points have been reached, is usually played out and the additional points added to the final score.

The five-point game is used in English whist. In addition to points from the seventh trick upwards, there are points for honours, revokes and winning games.

a) Four points are gained by partnerships holding all four honour cards, which are ace, K, Q and J of trumps. Two points are gained by holding any three honour cards.

Trick points take precedence over honour points if both partnerships reach a score of five points in the same deal. At the end of the game, the losers' honour points, if any, are discounted.

b) Revokes attract three penalty points, allotted according to one of the following alternative rulings, which must be agreed for the whole match:

i) three points are lost by the revoking couple;

ii) three points are gained by their opposition; or
iii) three points are transferred from the revokers to the opposition.
c) A game is declared when a partnership gains five points. The hand may be played out for additional points. The winners of the game get three extra points if opponents have a nil score; two if opponents have one or two points; and one if opponents have three or four points.

Winning the match

Three games make a rubber. If the first two games are won by the same partnership, the third game is not played. The partnership winning two games gets two extra points towards their final score.

The match is won by the partnership with the highest points total at the end of a rubber.

Beggar my neighbour

An exciting, easy game for two to six players in which winning depends largely on luck.

Cards

For two or three players, a standard deck of cards. It does not matter if a few cards are missing. Four or more players need approximately two packs.

Aim

To win all the cards in an agreed time limit.

Dealing

All the cards are dealt out one at a time; the deal might not be even. Nobody is allowed to look at their cards, which each player collects in a face-down pile.

Playing

The person on the dealer's left begins by placing his top card face up in the centre of the table. In turn, clockwise, each player adds a card to the centre pile until someone turns up an ace, J, Q or K (court card). The player so doing demands payment from the next player as follows:

a) for an ace: four cards
b) for a K: three cards
c) for a Q: two cards
d) for a J: one card

The payment cards are turned over and put on the central pile.

If a payment card is an ace or a court card, the next player has to pay the correct number of cards. This continues until payment is complete without aces or court cards. Then the last player who turned up a court card or ace takes the whole pile and adds it under his own. He then starts the next round with the next card in his pile.

Winning the game

The winner is the player who first goes out by using up all his cards. If nobody has gone out at the end of the time limit, the winner is the player with fewest cards.

Payments

 pay

 pay

 pay

 pay

Card dominoes

A game of skill and chance for two or more players,
also known as sevens, fan-tan or parliament.

Aim

Each person tries to be the first to add his cards in
sequence to a layout on the table.

Dealing

All 52 cards in a standard deck are dealt one at a time,
face down, to each player in clockwise order.

Playing

Players sort their own cards into sequences in each suit.
Whoever holds the 7 of diamonds begins play by
putting it face up on the table. In turn, clockwise,
players add a diamond card in sequence:

a) going up from 7 through 8, 9, 10, J, Q, K; or

b) going down from 7 through 6, 5, 4, 3, 2, ace.

A player can add a card to a sequence or start a new
sequence with another 7. If he cannot do either, he
passes and the turn goes to the next player.

Winning the game

The first player to use up all his cards is the winner but
the game goes on until everyone has played their cards
and completed the four sequences.

Example of play in progress

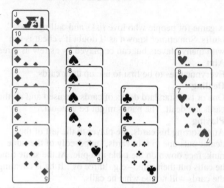

Cheat

A game for people who love risks and calling others'
bluffs. Sometimes known as 'I doubt it', cheat is fun
with many players but can be played by as few as three.

Aim

Everyone tries to be first to use up their cards.

Dealing

One or two standard decks of cards are used and all the
cards are dealt. The hands might be unequal.

Playing

After sorting his cards, the player to the left of the
dealer puts one to four cards, supposedly of the same
rank, face down on the table in a pile. At the same time
he calls out their rank – e.g. 'three 6s'. If he is cheating,
the cards will not be what he calls.

The players, in turn, play or pretend to play one to four
cards of the next higher rank.

Cheating

This can be done in two ways:

a) by putting down cards other than the ones he calls
(a player who cannot follow with the next higher rank
will have to pretend); or

b) by putting down more cards than he calls.

Calling someone's bluff

Anyone can challenge a player suspected of cheating
by calling, 'cheat' or 'I doubt it' before the next player
covers the cards.

When challenged, a player must turn up the cards he
played. If he was cheating, he has to pick up all the
cards played so far, but if he was not cheating, then the

challenger must pick them up. Whoever picks up the
pile starts the next round.

Winning the game

The winner is the person who manages to play his last
card without being challenged or his last card is
covered by the next player's cards before anyone
challenges.

UP-AND-DOWN CHEAT

Up-and-down cheat is a variation that allows players to
discard cards of the same or a lower rank than the
previous player's.

Donkey

A fast-moving, noisy game for three or more players.
Penalties are the letters of the word 'donkey'.

Aim

Each player tries to avoid losing six rounds of the game
and consequently becoming the donkey.

Cards

Although 'donkey' cards can be purchased, a standard
pack is frequently used.

A set is four cards with the same number or picture.
The number of sets needed is the same as the number
of players. For example, the aces, Ks, Qs, Js and 10s of
each suit would make the five sets needed for five
players.

The cards are well shuffled and dealt out so that each
player has four mixed cards.

Objects

Buttons, spoons or other non-breakables are needed.
One fewer objects than there are players are placed in
the middle before each round.

Playing

Everyone puts one card he does not want face down on
the table and slides it to the player on his left. Everyone
looks at the new card and decides whether to pass that
card on or change it for one from his hand before
passing it on.

This goes on very quickly until one player has a set of
four cards of the same value (four 10s, four Qs etc.).
This player quietly puts the set face down on the table
and picks up one of the objects. Immediately everyone

else tries to get an object. The one who fails loses and gets the D of donkey on the score sheet.

Donkey

The game is lost by the player who loses six rounds of the game and collects all the letters of donkey. His penalty is to 'hee-haw' for the other players.

PIG

This game is played the same way as donkey but without objects. Instead, the first player to collect a set of four cards puts his finger to his nose. The last player to do so becomes pig for that round. The first player to lose 10 rounds is called prize pig, loses the game and must say 'oink oink'.

Fish

A game of chance and skill for two, but better with more players. A standard deck of cards is used. A happy families pack may be preferred by younger players.

Aim

Players try to get rid of all their cards.

Dealing

If two or three are playing, each is dealt seven cards; if four or five, each gets five cards. The remaining cards are placed face down to form the stock, or fish pile.

Playing

Players sort their own cards into groups of the same rank (number or picture), keeping them hidden from the others.

The person on the left of the dealer asks anyone for cards of the same rank as one he holds. For example, if he holds the 6 of hearts in his hand he might say, 'John, give me your 6s.'

If 'John' has any, he must give them to the asker. The asker can then ask someone else for cards either of the same rank as the first or a different rank, as long as he holds one such card in his hand. He can go on asking for cards until a player does not have the card he wants. A player who does not have a card of the requested rank tells the asker to 'fish'. The person told to fish takes one card from the fish pile, and the person who said 'fish' continues the game by becoming the asker. Anyone who collects all four cards in a set puts them face down in front of him.

Winning the game

The winner is the first person to have no cards left
except a collection of sets. If two people run out of
cards together, the one with the most sets wins.

Sets are four cards of the same rank

Give away

An easy game for two or more players who enjoy speed
and alertness. A standard deck of cards is used.

Aim

Players try to be first to get rid of their cards.

Dealing

All the cards are dealt out, one at a time and face down,
without anyone seeing them. The cards stay face down
in a pile in front of each player. An unequal number of
cards in each hand does not matter.

Playing

The player on the dealer's left turns his top card over.
If it is an ace, he places it in the middle of the table and
turns another card over. If it is 2 of the same suit, he
adds it to the ace.

When a card is neither an ace nor a card that can be
added to any other face-up card, going up or down in
sequence, it is placed next to the player's own pile and
the turn passes to the next person clockwise.

Sequences are built in rank order ace, 2, 3, 4, 5, 6, 7, 8,
9, 10, J, Q, K. Cards can be added to the centre or to
any player's pile of upturned cards.

If a player's last card goes onto his own upturn pile, he
waits until his next turn to turn the pile over, face
down, and start again taking from the top.

If his last card goes into the centre or onto another's
pile, the player can immediately turn his pile over and
continue to play.

The winner is the one who is the first to discard all his cards either onto the centre pile or another player's upturn pile.

Play to centre

Play to own or other's face-up card

Go boom

A simple game for two or more players, which very young children can also enjoy. A standard deck of cards is used in which ace ranks high.

Aim

Everyone tries to get rid of all his cards first.

Dealing

Players cut; highest cut deals seven cards, one at a time, to each player clockwise.

The remaining cards are put face down in the centre of the table.

Playing

All players sort their cards and the person to the dealer's left starts the round by placing one of his cards face up on the table.

The next player, clockwise, adds a card that is:

a) the same suit (all hearts etc.); or

b) the same rank (number or picture) as the one before.

When a player cannot follow with one of the above, he picks cards from the spare pile until he gets a card he can play.

When everyone has played in that round, the person who played the highest ranking card starts the next round. If there is a tie, the one who played first starts the next round.

When the spare pile runs out, a player has to say 'pass' and it is the next player's turn.

Winning the game

The first to get rid of all his cards is the winner. He
proclaims this by shouting 'boom'.

SCORING GO BOOM

A variation in which points are scored for going boom,
making the game more complex. The player who goes
boom scores points for all the cards still held by the
other players, as follows:

a) K, Q and J: 10 points each
b) ace: 1 point each
c) all other cards: face value

The winner is the person first to score a number of
points that has been agreed, usually 250 points.

10 points each

1 point

CRAZY EIGHTS

This variation is played like go boom but using the 8s
as wild cards which can be played on any card. The
player of an 8 chooses which suit follows it.

The player who goes boom scores points for all the
cards still held by the other players, as follows:

a) 8:   50 points each
b) K, Q, J: 10 points each
c) ace: 1 point each

d) all other cards: face value

If the spare pile runs out before anyone goes boom, each player counts the value of his cards in hand and the winner is the one with the lowest total. The winner then scores the difference between his own total and the combined totals of the other players.

50 points   10 points   1 point

Knockout whist

A simple form of whist for two to seven players,
especially good for older children learning about tricks
and trumps. A deck of standard cards is used with aces
ranking high.

Rank

high   low

Aim

Everyone aims to win all the tricks of a hand and to
avoid being eliminated from the game.

Trump suit

At each deal one suit becomes the trump suit; cards of
that suit beat those of other suits.

Tricks

A trick is a group of cards, one played by each person
in turn. The suit of the first card played to a trick is
called the leading suit. The trick is won by the highest
card of the leading suit.

The highest cards are aces, then Ks, Qs, Js, 10s and so
on down to 3s and 2s.

If the leading suit is not the trump suit, a trump card

takes the trick.

| trump suit | trick won by Q clubs | trick won by 5 trumps |

Some tricks made by four players

Dealing

Clockwise, one person deals each player seven cards, one at a time and face down. The rest of the cards are piled face down in the centre of the table and the top card turned over. The suit of this card is trumps for that deal.

At each new deal players' hands have one fewer card.

Playing

Players sort their cards into suits in rank order. The player on the left of the dealer plays one card face up to start the first trick. The other players in turn add a card, following suit. If they cannot, they may use a trump card or play any other card.

The trick is won by the person who:

a) plays the highest trump card; or

b) by the highest card of the leading suit if trumps are not used. The winning player starts the next trick.

Play continues until all seven tricks have been made. Anyone who has not won a trick then drops out. The person winning the most tricks in the round begins the next round.

Winning the game
If a person wins all seven tricks in the first round, he is
the winner of the game. If all seven rounds of the game
are played, players have only one card in the last round.
The person winning this trick wins the game.

Linger longer

A good game for learning about trump cards. At least
three or more players are needed, but best with four or
six. A standard deck of cards is used, ace ranking high.

Rank

high   low

Aim

Players try to be the last left holding cards.

Trump suit

At each deal one suit becomes the trump suit; its cards
beat those of other suits.

Tricks

A trick is a group of cards, one played by each person
in turn. The suit of the first card played to a trick is the
leading suit. If no trumps are played, the trick is won
by the highest card of the leading suit.

The highest cards are aces, then Ks, Qs, Js, 10s and so
on down to 3s and 2s.

Dealing

One person deals cards, singly and face down, to each
player clockwise. Each person is dealt the same
number of cards as there are players. For example, six
players have six cards each.

The rest of the cards are piled face down on the table.

Some tricks made by four players

trumps   trick won by ace   trick won by
hearts   7 trumps

The dealer shows his last card to everyone and its suit
becomes the trump suit for the game.

Playing

The player on the dealer's left leads the trick by playing
one card face up. Everyone else plays one card to
complete the trick.

Cards should follow the suit of the first card; otherwise
a trump card or any other card can be played.

The trick is won by the person who:

a) plays the highest trump card; or

b) by the highest card of the leading suit if trumps are
not used.

The winning player collects his trick near him, takes a
card from the stock pile and uses any of his cards to
start the next trick.

Players continue as long as they have cards in their hand.

A player whose hand runs out drops out of the game.

The winner is the last person in the game.

Memory

Also known as pelmanism or concentration. this is a
simple game of observation and memory for any
number of players.

Aim

Everyone tries to collect as many cards as he can.

Cards

One standard deck of cards is needed for two or three
players; two decks woud be better for more players.
The cards should be fairly new and clean so they look
alike from the back and do not give away clues about
their identity by being torn or creased. A large flat area
is needed for playing, such as the floor or a large table.

Dealing

One person shuffles the cards and places them all face
down and separate, so they are not touching.

Playing

The player on the dealer's left turns over any two cards
so that all players can see them.

If they are the same rank, such as two Ks or two 5s, he
keeps them and turns over two more cards.

The player continues in this way until the two cards do
not match. Then he leaves them exactly where they
were, face down. The next player clockwise then has
a turn.

If a player turns a card up the same rank as one that has
already been turned and replaced, he must try to
remember where it was, hoping to make a pair.

Play continues until all the cards have been taken. The
player with the most cards is the winner.

Menagerie

Also called animals, this game is for two or more
players, the more the better. It is great fun and very
noisy. Two standard decks of cards are used.

Aim

Each player tries to win all the cards.

Choosing animals

Each player chooses an animal name that is long and
hard to say. These names are written on small pieces of
paper, which are folded and shaken up together in a hat
or box. Each player takes one and has that animal for
the game. Everyone then learns the names of all the
animals.

Dealing

All the cards are dealt clockwise, one at a time and face
down. The hands might be unequal. A player must not
look at his cards but put them in a face-down pile.

Playing

The player on the left of the dealer turns his top card
over to begin his face-up pile. Each does the same in
turn.

When a player notices that another face-up card is the
same rank (same number or picture) as his face-up
card, he must shout out the name of the other player's
animal three times.

The first player to correctly shout out wins the other
player's face-up pile, adding them to the bottom of his
own face-down pile.

If a player calls the wrong name, he must give all his
face-up cards to the player whose name he shouted.

A player wins when he has collected all the cards.

My ship sails

Easy to learn, this game is exciting when played at high speed. It is for four to seven players using one standard deck of cards, ace ranking high.

Aim

Players try to collect seven cards from the same suit, such as seven hearts.

Dealing

The dealer is the person who cuts the highest card.
Seven cards are dealt to each player, one at a time and face down, clockwise. The rest of the deck is not needed.

Playing

Players sort their cards by suits. They decide which suit to collect, although these can change as cards are exchanged.

Exchanging

Each person puts an unwanted card face down on the table and slides it to the player on the right, who picks it up. Each then discards another card, slides it to the right and picks up his own new card from the left.
This continues until one player's hand is all one suit and he shouts 'My ship sails'. The first to do so is the winner.

My ship sails

Old maid

An easy game for three or more young children, also
called 'pass the lady'.

Aim

There are no winners. Instead, players try to avoid
being the loser by getting rid of all their cards.

Cards

A standard deck of 52 cards is used with one of the Qs
removed. This leaves a deck with a pair of Qs in one
colour and a single Q – the old maid – in the other.

Old maid

one Q
removed

old maid

pair of Qs

Dealing

All the cards are dealt, face down and one at a time.
Hands might be unequal.

Playing

Players sort their cards, keeping them hidden from
other players. Anyone holding pairs of matching cards
puts them out face up. Pairs are two cards with the
same number or picture.

If someone holds three matching cards, he only puts
down one pair and keeps the odd card. If he has four,
he puts down two pairs.

The player to the left of the dealer spreads his cards in his hand, keeping them hidden. He offers them to the player on his left who takes one card. If the card matches one already held, he puts down the pair. If not, he puts it in his hand, and he in turn spreads his cards for the player on his left.

The game continues in the same way until all the cards have been put down in pairs except the old maid, which cannot be paired. The person holding the card is called 'old maid' by the others and loses the game.

VARIATIONS

The French game is called le vieux garçon (old boy), which is the J of spades. All the other Js are removed from the deck.

Another version requires pairs to be matched for colour as well as number, such as a pair of red aces or a pair of black 10s.

Le vieux garçon

three Js removed

J of spades is the old boy

Pairs

Play or pay

A game using rank and sequence for three or more
players. It is also called round the corner.

Aim

Players try to win counters by getting rid of their cards
in each round.

Dealing

Each deal is one round of the game. Players should
agree how many rounds will make the game.

One player deals all the cards clockwise from a
standard deck, one at a time and face down. Players
might not have equal numbers.

Each player also starts with 20 counters.

Playing

The player on the dealer's left plays one card face up.
The next player, on his left, looks to see if he can
follow that card with one in the same suit in sequence:
ace, 2, 3, 4, 5, 6, 7, 8, 9, 10, J, Q, K.

If the card played is the K, the sequence goes 'round
the corner' to the ace of that suit.

If a player holds the next card in sequence, he plays it
face up on top of the last card. If he does not, he must
pay one counter into the middle of the table.

The person playing the last card of a suit then plays any
card from his hand to start the next one.

Winning the game

The winner of the round is the first person to play all
his cards. He takes all the counters from the centre.
Losers each pay him one counter for every card they
still hold.

The winner of the game is the person with the most counters after the agreed number of rounds.

Cards in sequence

Each deal is one round of the game. Players should agree how many rounds will make up the game.

One player deals all the cards clockwise from a standard deck, one at a time until they are all gone. Some players spread the cards.

Each player then starts with 10 counters.

Playing

The play is on the table. The player nearest the dealer starts by putting his hand face up in front of him and whoever holds the ace of clubs plays it.

The next card played is the two, the sequence going round the circle, and the player holding the next card in sequence plays it on the pile if he can. If he does not he must pay one counter into the middle of the table.

The person playing the last card of a suit then plays any card from his hand to start the next suit.

Winning the game

The winner of the round is the first person to play all his cards. He takes all the counters from the centre. The losers each pay further counters for every card they still hold.

Racing demon

A noisy game for any number that is played at great
speed and requires a lot of space.

Aim

Players try to use all 13 cards in their piles and play as
many cards as they can into the middle.

Cards

Each player needs a complete deck of 52 cards. Old
cards with different backs are the best.

Dealing

Players shuffle their own decks and deal themselves 13
cards face down. The pile is turned up and four more
cards are dealt face up side by side with it. Players
keep their remaining cards face down in one hand.

Playing

One person is the starter who shouts 'go' to start the
game once everyone has dealt. Players put cards into
the centre or on their own row of four cards as fast as
they can.

Playing into the centre

If a player has an ace, this should be put face up in the
centre. The 2 of the same suit, followed by the 3, 4, 5,
6, 7, 8, 9, 10, J, Q, K in that order, can then be played
by the person holding them.

Playing onto the four face-up cards

Each player can play onto his own row of four cards
but must play in descending order, alternating black
and red cards. For example, red K, black Q, or black 9,
red 8, black 7 and so on.

Which cards can be played

a) The top card from the 13 pile.

b) A card or a sequence of cards from one of any other face-up piles. Gaps made by doing this are filled with the top card from the pile of 13.

c) If neither of the above is possible, the player turns three cards over from the spare pile in his hand to make a new face-up pile. This is continued until the player gets a card he can play. When the spare pile runs out, the face-up pile is turned over to use as a spare pile.

Ending the game

A player shouts 'out' as soon as he has used up all the cards from his original pile of 13.

Scoring

The cards from the centre are sorted into their different decks. Each player counts how many cards are left in his original face-up piles. His final score is this number subtracted from the number from his deck in the centre. The player with the highest score is the winner.

Rolling stone

A popular game with unexpected moments for four, five or six players.

Aim

Players try to get rid of their cards.

Cards

One standard deck is used with the 2s removed for six players; 2s, 3s and 4s removed for five; and 2s, 3s, 4s, 5s, and 6s, removed for four. Aces rank high.

Rank

high   low

Dealing

Players cut; highest cut deals all the cards clockwise, one at a time, so that each player has eight cards.

Playing

Players sort their cards by suit. The player to the left of the dealer plays one card face up. The next player on his left must play a card of the same suit (follow suit). Each player in turn plays one card following suit and the group of cards, or trick, is piled face down. The person who played the highest card starts the next round. If a player cannot follow suit, he picks up all the cards played for that trick, adding them to his hand. He starts the next trick from the cards he already held.

The player to run out of cards first is the winner.

Sequence

Easy to learn, this game uses some skill. Best with four or five players, but as few as two can play.

Aim

Players try to get rid of their cards, and collect counters, by playing on sequences.

Cards

A standard deck of cards is used. Cards are ranked in numerical order: 2, 3, 4, 5, 6, 7, 8, 9, 10, J, Q, K, ace. Cards all of the same suit make up a sequence.

A sequence

high   low

Dealing

One player deals the whole deck one at a time, face down and clockwise. Some players may hold unequal numbers of cards. Each player also begins with 10 counters, and the number of rounds is agreed.

Playing

The player to the dealer's left plays his lowest card face up on the table. The player who holds the next card (or cards) in sequence plays it.

Play continues until all the cards of that sequence have been played, from the 2 up to the ace. The next sequence is begun by whoever played the last card. The winner is the player who is first to get rid of all his cards.

Scoring

At the end of a round, the losers pay the winner one counter for every card they hold. The winner of the game is the one with the most counters after all the rounds.

Slap jack

An easy, exciting game for two or more players, and very good for young children.

Aim

Everyone tries to win all the cards. The game can be played with or without a time limit.

Cards

A deck of standard cards is used. Two decks can be mixed if more than three play, and if some cards are missing it is not important.

Dealing

The whole deck is dealt by one person, face down and one at a time in clockwise direction. Players must not look at their cards, which they put in piles in front of them. Some might have more than others.

Playing

The player to the left of the dealer turns his top card over and places it face up in the centre. Then the player to his left does the same.

Play continues like this until someone plays a J. Then every player tries to be first to put his hand on it and 'slap the jack'. The one who does so gets the whole pile of cards, shuffles them with his own and piles them face down to use. The player to his left starts the next round.

If two people slap the J, the winner is the one with his hand underneath.

If someone loses all his cards, he has one chance to stay in the game by being the first to slap the J on the next round. If he fails, he must drop out of the game.

Penalty

When someone slaps the wrong card, he must give his next card to the player whose card he slapped.

Winning the game

The game is won when:

a) a player collects all the cards; or

b) a player holds the most cards at the end of an agreed time limit.

Snap

A very popular, noisy game of great fun for two or more players.

Aim

Everyone tries to take all the cards.

Cards

An old, standard deck is fun to use, although special snap cards are available. Two decks are better for more than three players. If some are missing, it does not matter.

Dealing

All the cards are dealt out by one player, singly and face down in a clockwise direction. Players do not look at their cards. It does not matter if some players have more than others. Everyone piles their cards in front of them, face down.

Playing

The player on the left of the dealer turns his top card over and puts it face down next to his own pile. The next player on his left does the same, making another upturned pile of his own. All the other players do the same in turn. When a player runs out of face-down cards he turns his face-up pile down and continues.

Snap

When one player sees that the cards on top of two piles match, such as two 8s or two Ks, he shouts 'snap!' The first to do so collects both the piles which have the matched cards and adds them to the bottom of his own face-down pile.

Play continues with the person to the left of the last person to turn over a card.

Snap

The snap pool

When two players shout snap at the same time, the two piles of cards are placed together in the centre and are called the snap pool.

Play continues as before. When someone turns up a card that matches the card on top of the pool, he shouts 'snap pool!' and takes the whole pool.

Penalty

Everyone should agree which penalty is to be paid when a player incorrectly calls snap:

a) the player pays each person one card from his face-down pile; or

b) the player's face-down pile is turned over, placed in the centre and becomes a snap pool.

The winner is the one player left with cards.

EASY SNAP

Very good for young children, this variation has only one, central face-up pile. Snap is shouted when the top two cards match.

SPEED SNAP

This version is very fast-moving because everyone turns their cards over at the same time instead of in turn.

Snip-snap-snorem

A fast, hilarious game for three or more players using a standard deck of cards.

Aim

Everyone tries to get rid of his cards.

Dealing

Players cut; highest cut is the dealer. Ace is high in this game.

All the cards are dealt one at a time, face down and clockwise. Some players may have more than others.

Playing

Players sort their cards, putting together cards that match each other in order, such as two 4s, a 5, four 6s, one 7, two 10s, three Js and so on.

The player to the left of the dealer plays one card face up in the centre.

If the next player to the left has a card that matches, he puts it down and shouts 'snip!' If he has another matching card he must wait for his next turn to play it. If he cannot play a card he says 'pass'.

Play continues in turn, clockwise, until a player puts the third matching card in the centre. He shouts 'snap!' The player to put down the fourth matching card shouts 'snorem!' He then starts the next round.

Winning the game

The first player to get rid of all his cards is the winner.

Variation

When a player has two or more matching cards, he plays them all together, shouting 'snip snap' or 'snip snap snorem'.

Sample play

Snip!   Snap!   Snorem!

JIG

This is played the same as snip snap snorem, but players put down sequences of four cards which can be from different suits, for example 5, 6, 7, 8. The players shout 'jiggety, joggety, jig!' when they play each card.

Spit

A fast-moving game for two people who enjoy being alert. A standard deck of cards is used.

Aim

Both players try to get rid of all their cards.

Dealing

All the cards are dealt equally, one at a time, to each player. Players put down cards in front of them as follows:

a) beginning from the left, three cards are placed face down in a row, then a fourth card is placed face up;

b) beginning from the left again, another face-down card is placed on the first and second cards and a face-up card on the third;

c) a face-down card is then placed on the first pile and a face-up card on the second;

d) finally a face-up card is placed on the first pile.

Players put their remaining cards in a pile, face down to the left of their rows.

Playing

When both are ready, one player shouts 'spit!' Both players take the top card from their spare pile and put them face up in the centre, next to each other.

Playing to the centre

With as much speed as possible, both players play as many cards from their face-up rows as they can onto the centre cards.

The card must be in sequence, up or down. For example, if the centre card is 10, then a J or 9 can be put on it (a 2 or a K can be played onto an ace). If a face-down card is revealed, it is turned up.

Spit

Play continues in this way until neither can lay down any more cards on the centre. When this happens, one of them shouts 'spit!' Both players put a card from the top of their spare pile face up onto the central pile they started.

Play then continues. If neither can continue, one shouts 'spit' again and they each put another card on the centre from their spare piles. If a player's spare pile runs out and he wants to call spit, he turns his central pile over, shouts 'spit' and continues to play using it as a spare pile.

Ending a round

A player should shout 'out' as soon as he has played all the cards from his face-up row. He wins the round.

He picks up his spare pile, and the other player picks up both central piles and the cards left in his row, adding them under his spare pile.

Starting another round

Both players lay down a row of cards as in the first round. Play continues in the same way as before with one exception. After the first round, if a player's spare pile runs out he plays without it and both people play onto the same pile in the centre.

Winning the game

The first player to get rid of all his cards wins the game.

Stealing bundles

Also called stealing the old man's bundle, this game is
for two to four players using one standard deck of
cards. Young children able to match cards of the same
rank will enjoy it.

Aim

Players try to collect the most cards.

Dealing

One player deals each player four cards, singly and
face down in a clockwise direction. The next four cards
are then put face up in a row in the centre. The rest of
the deck is put face down to one side.

Playing

The player to the left of the dealer looks to see if he has
a card that matches in rank one in the centre. If he has,
he captures the centre card and puts it face up with his
own near him. This is his 'bundle'.

If a player's card is the same rank as two or three
centre cards, he can capture them all at the same time.

If a player's card is the same rank as the top card in
somebody's bundle, he can capture the whole bundle.

If none of a player's cards matches any centre card he
must 'trail', or put one of his own cards face up in the
centre.

Everyone plays a card in turn. Whenever cards are
captured, they are put on the bundle with the matching
card face up.

Cards of the same rank

Extra deals

When everyone has played all of his four cards, four
more cards are dealt to each player, and none to the
centre, and the game continues.

Winning the game

When all the cards have been dealt and played, the
player with the most cards in his bundle wins.

War

An easy introduction to card playing, war is for two
players using a standard deck of cards. It can be varied
for three players.

Aim

Everyone tries to get all the cards.

Dealing

One person deals the whole deck one at a time face
down. Both players put their cards face down in a pile
without looking at them.

Playing

Each player turns over the top card of his pile and puts
it in the centre face up next to the other player's card.
The player whose card is the higher ranking, regardless
of suit, collects both cards and adds them to the bottom
of his pile.

Players continue to turn over cards together and collect
them.

Rank of cards in mixed suits

high   low

War

War occurs when two cards of the same rank are turned
over.

Both players then put another card on top of their first

card, but face down, and another face up. The higher ranking of the last two cards wins all six cards.

If these are the same rank, the war continues, and the player turning up the higher ranking card will claim 10 or more cards from the centre.

Playing war

player A

player B

player A wins all six cards

Winning the game

The game is won by:

a) the player who wins all the cards; or

b) the player with the most cards at the end of an agreed time limit.

War for three players

Played as for two players except:

a) the last card is not dealt out, so all players have the same number;

b) when any two cards of the same rank are turned

over, all three people play war;

c) when all three turned-up cards are the same rank, everyone plays double war;

d) when playing double war everyone puts two cards face down to one card face up, and if the cards match they continue with single war.

PERSIAN PASHA

In this variation, players turn over their top cards and begin a face-up pile next to their face-down pile. Both players turn over cards until they have a match, when the player of the higher-ranking card wins the other's entire face-up pile.